AGES
9+

GUINNESS WORLD RECORDS

BizaRRe!

FUN FACTS & ACTIVITIES

D1473453

AMERICAN
EDUCATION
PUBLISHING™

American Education Publishing™
An imprint of Carson-Dellosa Publishing LLC
Greensboro, North Carolina

©2012 Guinness World Records Limited

Visit Guinness World Records at
guinnessworldrecords.com

Carson-Dellosa Publishing LLC
P.O. Box 35665
Greensboro, NC 27425 USA

ISBN 978-1-60996-892-2   01-153121151

Photo: Guinness World Records Limited

Photo: Guinness World Records Limited

WHAT'S INSIDE?

Photo: Guinness World Records Limited

CAUTION CAUTION CAUTION

A Note to the Reader of This Book

Inside this book, you will find facts about unusual objects and creatures, epic journeys, and thrilling feats. Read and enjoy the stories, but never try to set a world record on your own! Breaking records can be dangerous and even life threatening. If you think you have a good idea for a safe, record-breaking event, talk to an adult. You can learn more about how to set a world record at guinnessworldrecords.com.

Throughout this book, you will find activity ideas that encourage you to learn more, get active, use your brain, be creative, and have fun. Try all the activities, but pause and think before you do each one. Ask yourself: What should I do to be safe and follow the rules? Do I need a parent's permission to go somewhere or to use materials? Always ask an adult if you are unsure.

Now, turn to any page. Get ready to be amazed by Guinness World Records® facts!

CAUTION CAUTION CAUTION

Photo: Guinness World Records Limited

AMAZING BODIES

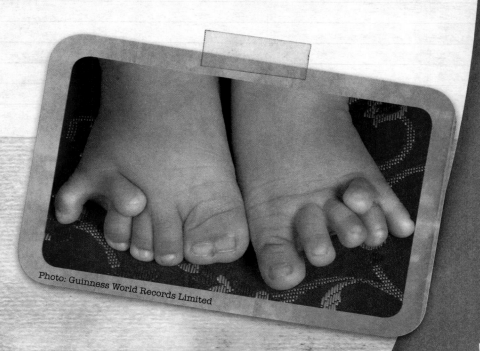

Photo: Guinness World Records Limited

Furthest Eyeball Pop

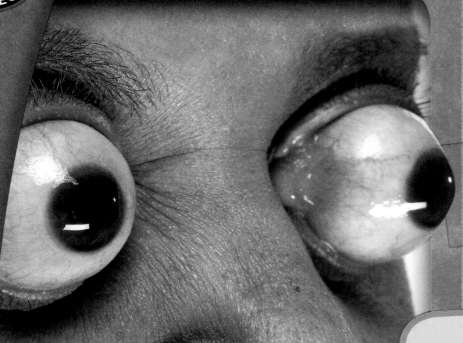

On November 2, 2007, Kim Goodman (USA) popped her eyeballs 0.47 in. (12 mm) beyond her eye sockets.

Photo: Guinness World Records Limited

Did You Know?
The Atlantic giant squid has the largest eyes of any animal. One eye is about the size of a dinner plate!

ACTIVITIES

1. Find something that is about one-half inch long. What did you find? Draw it here.

2. How many seconds can you hold your eyes open without blinking? Ask a friend to time you.

_____

3. Have a staring contest with a friend. Who won?

_____

Furthest Distance to Pull a Single-Decker Bus With the Ears

Photo: Guinness World Records Limited

On March 31, 2008, Manjit Singh (UK) pulled a single-decker bus 20 ft. (6.1 m) with his ears in Loughborough, United Kingdom, to raise money for a fitness center.

Did You Know?
Your ears and nose will continue to grow during your lifetime, but your eyes will not.

ACTIVITIES

1. Objects in motion tend to stay in motion. Use a jump rope to play tug-of-war with a friend. What happens when your friend tugs you? Is it difficult to stop moving forward?

   _____

2. Use sidewalk chalk (outside) or masking tape (inside) to make a line that is 20 feet long. Run, skip, and hop along the line. What did you do?

   _____

Longest Chest Hair

Photo: Guinness World Records Limited

On April 29, 2007, Richard Condo's (USA) chest hair was 9 in. (22.8 cm) long.

Did You Know?

Once a hair pops through the skin, it is no longer alive, which is why it doesn't hurt to cut it.

ACTIVITIES

1. Write one reason that having hair is helpful to humans and other mammals.

_____

2. Human hair grows from holes in the skin called *follicles*. Round follicles produce straight hair, while curly hair grows out of oval-shaped follicles. Similarly, larger follicles are associated with thicker hair, while fine hair comes from smaller follicles. Think about the hair on your head. Circle adjectives that describe your follicles.

round   **oval**   **larger**   **smaller**

Longest Arm Hair

Photo: Guinness World Records Limited

On October 7, 2009, Justin Shaw's (USA) arm hair measured 5.75 in. (14.61 cm) long in Miami, Florida.

Did You Know?

Hair grows on every part of your outer body except on the palms of your hands, the soles of your feet, your eyelids, and your lips.

ACTIVITIES

1. Circle adjectives that describe the hair on your head.

springy	fine	shiny
heavy	lengthy	straight
bright	soft	short

2. Have you ever felt your hair "stand on end"? Goose bumps happen when tiny muscles at the base of your hair follicles contract. Write about something that gave you goose bumps.

_____

Furthest Milk Squirting Distance

Photo: Guinness World Records Limited

On September 1, 2004, Ilker Yilmaz (Turkey) squirted milk from his eye a distance of 9 ft. 2 in. (2.795 m) at the Armada Hotel, Istanbul, Turkey.

Did You Know?
Yilmaz has to suck milk through his nose before he can squirt it from his eye!

CHECK THIS OUT!

Some Guinness World Records attract a lot of competition. For example, many people try to be the fastest or strongest. Other records are just weird. What Ilker Yilmaz (Turkey) does is one of the weird ones. He can squirt milk out of his eye!

For years, Yilmaz knew that he had this ability. He discovered it as a boy, while he was swimming. He noticed water would squirt out of his eye. Years passed. Then, one day he saw a man on TV. The man was trying to set a record for squirting liquid out of his eye. Yilmaz thought, "Maybe, I could do that, too." Three years later, Yilmaz set a new world record.

ACTIVITIES

1. Can you find Turkey on a map of the world? Write the names of other countries you find that start with the letter *T*.

   T_____   T_____

   T_____   T_____

2. Milk and other dairy foods are a good source of calcium. Circle your favorite dairy foods.

yogurt	**ice cream**	**string cheese**
pudding	**frozen yogurt**	**cheddar cheese cubes**
milk	**cottage cheese**	**smoothies**

3. Fill in vowel letters to complete a word you read on page 10.

   c ☐ mp ☐ t ☐ t ☐ ☐ n

   Circle the definition that best fits the word.

   a. curiosity about what is happening

   b. disinterest; not caring one way or another

   c. struggling to win or come out first

   d. winning easily, without much effort

4. With help from an adult, pour 2% or whole milk in a bowl and allow it to come to room temperature. Put in a few drops of food coloring, then a drop of dish soap. What happens? Describe it.

   _____

   _____

   _____

Longest Spaghetti Nasal Ejection

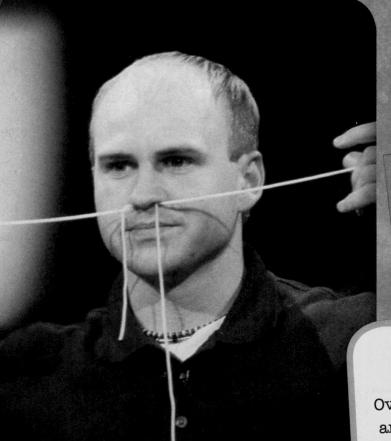

Photo: Guinness World Records Limited

On December 16, 1998, Kevin Cole (USA) successfully blew a strand of spaghetti out of his nose over a distance of 7.5 in. (19 cm) on the set of *Guinness World Records: Primetime* in Los Angeles, California.

Did You Know?
Over a million pounds of pasta are sold in American grocery stores each year.

ACTIVITIES

1. Use dry spaghetti to make a bridge between stacks of blocks or books. What object does your bridge support? How can you make it stronger?

_____

_____

2. Can you make a cotton ball or a scrap of paper move by blowing on it through your nose? How far can you move it?

_____

Longest Time to Hold Breath Voluntarily (Female)

Photo: Guinness World Records Limited

On July 10, 2009, Karoline Mariechen Meyer (Brazil) held her breath under water for 18 minutes 32.59 seconds in Florianopolis, Brazil.

Did You Know?
The hairs on the inside of your nose help to clean the air as you breathe.

ACTIVITIES

1. You can increase your lung capacity with regular exercise. Write your four favorite ways to play and exercise.

   _____   _____

   _____   _____

2. Most kids breathe 16-30 times per minute. Count your breaths for 30 seconds, then multiply by 2. Write the number of times you breathe per minute.

   _____

Most Concrete Blocks Broken With the Elbow While Holding a Raw Egg

On March 6, 2010, Christopher Læret (Norway) broke a total of 14 concrete blocks with his elbow while holding an uncooked egg without breaking it.

Photo: Guinness World Records Limited

Did You Know?
Most people cannot lick their own elbows. Try it!

ACTIVITIES

1. A bubble is fragile like an egg. Blow a soap bubble and hold it in your hand. How many times can you jump without breaking it?

_____

2. What else can you do with a bubble in your hand?

_____

3. Breaking 14 concrete blocks set this record. How many groups of 14 are in 168?

_____

Most Pierced Woman

Photo: Guinness World Records Limited

As of June 8, 2006, Elaine Davidson (UK) had 4,225 body piercings. Her piercings are located all over her body, including places such as her ears, forehead, eyebrows, chin, nose, and tongue.

Did You Know?

The earliest known body piercing was seen on a mummified Egyptian man who lived more than 5,000 years ago.

ACTIVITIES

Draw a wacky earring in each pierced ear.

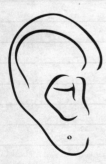

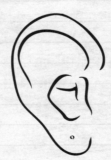

Loudest Burp (Male)

Photo: Guinness World Records Limited

Paul Hunn (UK) let out a burp that reached 109.9 decibels on August 23, 2009, at a live Guinness World Records event in Bognor Regis, United Kingdom.

Did You Know?
Cows burp about 50 million tons of gas into the air each year.

CHECK THIS OUT!

Paul Hunn (United Kingdom) holds the record for the world's Loudest Burp by a Male. But can a female burp louder?

On June 16, 2009, about 30,000 people were watching a burping contest, a popular event in Italy that raises money for charity. They had no idea that they would see and hear a new Guinness World Record. Elisa Cagnoni (Italy) let out a burp that was 107.0 decibels. Cagnoni won the contest and also set a world record for the Loudest Burp by a Female.

So, how loud are these world record burps? A blowing car horn measures 110 decibels, and a rock concert is about 120 decibels. That's pretty loud!

1. On April 16, 1994, Annalisa Wray (United Kingdom) shouted the word *quiet*. Her voice reached 121.7 dB (decibels). How much louder was Wray's shout than Hunn's burp?

   a. 11.8 dB

   b. 11.0 dB

   c. 10.9 dB

   d. 11.82 dB

2. Your ears are incredibly sensitive. They can hear everything from a soft footstep to a jet engine. *Decibels* measure the intensity of sound. It's important to protect your ears. Sounds above 85 dB can cause hearing loss with prolonged exposure. Fill in the chart by writing the sounds from softest to loudest.

   lawn mower: 90 dB   **rock concert: 120 dB**

   whisper: 15 dB   **normal talking: 60 dB**

   firecracker: 140 dB

Sounds: Softest to Loudest	Decibels (dB)
1.	
2.	
3.	
4.	
5.	

3. In some parts of the world, it is polite to burp after a meal. Do you think burping is rude? Explain why or why not.

   _____

   _____

Smallest Waist (Living Person)

Photo: Guinness World Records Limited

Cathie Jung (USA) has a corseted waist measuring 15 in. (38.1 cm).

Did You Know?

The first corsets were uncomfortable, made from iron, wood, and even whalebone! At one time, both boys and girls wore them.

ACTIVITIES

Use a tape measure to measure around your body parts in inches. Fill in the chart below. Use the last column to rank the measurements from 1 (largest) to 4 (smallest).

Body Part	Inches	Rank
wrist		
waist		
head		
big toe		

Longest Legs (Female)

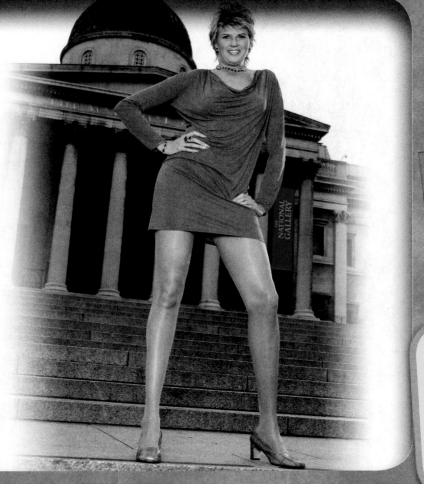

Photo: Guinness World Records Limited

Svetlana Pankratova's (Russia) legs are 4 ft. 4 in. (1.32 m) long.

Did You Know?
Your thighbone, or femur, is stronger than concrete.

ACTIVITIES

1. What special things could you do if you had extra long legs or arms?

_____

_____

2. Your legs are amazing! Circle your favorite ways to use your legs.

kick	bike	dance
run	jump	skip
walk	swim	climb

Most Tattooed Person

Photo: Guinness World Records Limited

Lucky Diamond Rich (Australia) had 100 percent of his skin tattooed with black ink, including his eyelids, the skin between his toes, down into his ears, and his gums.

Did You Know?
Lucky Diamond Rich is now layering white tattoos on top of the black, and colorful tattoos on top of the white.

ACTIVITIES

Cover this hand with tattoos. Choose pictures and words that are meaningful to you.

Tallest Girl

Photo: Guinness World Records Limited

On January 16, 2009, Malee Duangdee (Thailand) measured 6 ft. 10 in. (2.08 m) tall in Bangkok, Thailand.

Did You Know?

When Malee was just 12 years old, she was already 6 ft. 2 in. (1.87 m) tall, nearly a foot taller than her father.

ACTIVITIES

1. Give Duangdee's height in inches.

_____

2. Ask a friend to measure your height. How many inches tall are you?

_____

3. Compare your height to Duangdee's. How many inches taller is Duangdee?

_____

Longest Hair (Female)

Photo: Guinness World Records Limited

On May 8, 2004, Xie Qiuping's (China) hair was 18 ft. 5.54 in. (5.627 m) long. She has been growing her hair since 1973.

Did You Know?
Hair grows more quickly during the day and in the summer than during the night and in the winter.

CHECK THIS OUT!

Xie Qiuping (China) holds the record for the longest hair for any woman in the world. Xie Qiuping started growing her hair long in 1973 when she was 13 years old. She did not cut her hair for more than 35 years!

Hair grows well only when you have a healthy body and diet. Long hair also requires a lot of care to wash and brush, but Xie Qiuping insists that her hair is not a burden. "It's no trouble at all," she says.

Xie Qiuping sometimes wears her hair tied up. Other times, she lets it all down. When she wears her hair loose, she needs an assistant to hold it so that it does not drag on the ground.

ACTIVITIES

Complete the crossword puzzle with words you read on page 22.

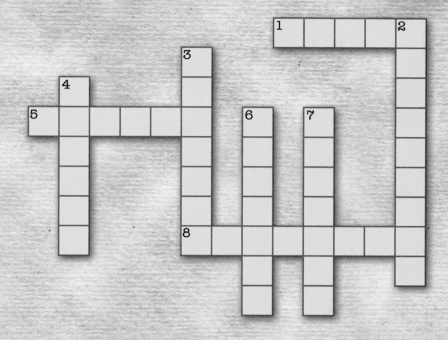

Across

1. Country where Xie Qiuping lives

5. Although Xie Qiuping's hair requires a lot of care, she says it is not a _____.

8. Age when Xie Qiuping began to grow her long hair

Down

2. Person who helps Xie Qiuping hold her loose hair off the ground

3. Xie Qiuping holds the record for the _____ hair (female).

4. Season of the year when hair tends to grow faster

6. In Chinese names, the family name comes first and the given name is last. What is Xie Qiuping's given name?

7. This type of diet helps hair grow well

Largest Gape

J. J. Bittner (USA) can open his mouth to a gape of 3.4 in. (8.4 cm).

Photo: Guinness World Records Limited

Did You Know?
Your mandible, or jawbone, holds your lower teeth and is the largest and strongest bone of your face.

ACTIVITIES

1. How wide can you open your mouth? Use a ruler to take a measurement and write it here.

_____

2. One meaning of *gape* is "to gaze in openmouthed surprise or wonder." Write about something that could make you gape.

_____

_____

Heaviest Weight Lifted by a Human Beard

Photo: Guinness World Records Limited

On September 16, 2007, Antanas Kontrimas (Lithuania) lifted a 139-lb. 5.3-oz. (63.2 kg) girl with his beard in Beijing, China.

Did You Know?

Hair is so strong that a whole head of it could support the weight of two elephants!

ACTIVITIES

1. Get a blade of grass, a human hair, and a thread. Break each in two. Which material was strongest? Which was weakest?

   _____

2. Use a bathroom scale to weigh yourself. How much do you weigh?

   _____

3. Use the bathroom scale to weigh all kinds of things. Try a box of cereal, shoes, or a book. What was heaviest? Lightest?

   _____

Most Fingers and Toes on a Living Person

Photo: Guinness World Records Limited

Both Pranamya Menaria (India) and Devendra Harne (India) have a total of 25 fingers and toes. They each have 12 fingers and 13 toes as a result of the condition polydactylism.

Did You Know?
An artificial big toe was found on the foot of an ancient Egyptian mummy.

ACTIVITIES

Breaking a long word into parts can help you understand its meaning. *Polydactylism* is made from these word parts:

poly (many) + *dactyl* (finger or toe) + *ism* (condition) = *polydactylism*

Write long words made from these parts:

tri (three) + *cerat* (horn) + *ops* (face) = _____

in (not) + *cred* (believe) + *ible* (able) = _____

Most Eggs Crushed With the Head in One Minute

Photo: Guinness World Records Limited

On April 24, 2010, Leo Mondello (Italy) crushed 130 eggs with his head in one minute in Patti, Messina, Italy.

Did You Know?

It takes a hen 24 to 26 hours to make an egg. In 30 minutes, she can start another!

ACTIVITIES

1. How many eggs could Mondello crush with his head in three minutes?

   _____

2. A hen lays about five eggs each week. How many eggs can a hen lay in a year?

   _____

3. How many eggs will three hens lay in two weeks?

   _____

Photo: Guinness World Records Limited

Kevin Shelley (USA) broke 46 wooden toilet seats with his head in one minute in Cologne, Germany, on September 1, 2007.

Did You Know?
Jewelry designer Sydney Mobell created a $400,000 gold toilet seat with gems on its lid.

CHECK THIS OUT!

Kevin Shelley (United States) teaches elementary school. He helps students use their heads to learn. When he is not in the classroom, he uses his head another way. He breaks toilet seats with it!

Shelley has practiced martial arts for more than 20 years. So, he knows how to be safe when he uses his head. Kevin's board-breaking technique is to take the boards and hit them over his head. As one half of the board flies backwards, he drops what is left in front of him. He didn't even get a headache after setting the record!

1. How much time did it take Shelley to break each toilet seat? Write your answer in the boxes. Round to the nearest tenth.

☐ . ☐

2. Dentists recommend that you brush your teeth for two minutes. How many toilet seats could Shelley break in the time it takes you to brush your teeth? Write your answer in the boxes.

☐ ☐

3. The average person visits the bathroom 2,500 times each year. How many times will you go to the bathroom in four years? Write your answer in the boxes.

☐ ☐ , ☐ ☐ ☐

4. Some words that mean "room with a toilet" are *powder room*, *lavatory*, and *water closet*. Can you think of others? Write them on the lines.

_____   _____

5. If Shelley broke about one toilet seat every 1.3 seconds, how many did he break in 10.4 seconds? Complete the table below.

Number of Toilet Seats	1							
Time (sec.)	1.3							10.4

Most Clothespins Clipped on a Face

Photo: Guinness World Records Limited

Garry Turner (UK) clipped 160 clothespins to his face on January 9, 2009, in Madrid, Spain.

Did You Know?
Clothespins have been around for a long time. In the 1800s, 146 different kinds of clothespins were patented.

ACTIVITIES

1. Using a clothesline instead of an electric dryer can save a family $100 each year in energy costs. If 10 neighbors used clotheslines, how much would be saved in one year?

_____

2. Some people love clotheslines because they save energy. Others think they are ugly and should not be used. What do you think?

_____

_____

Longest Time to Hula-Hoop Under Water

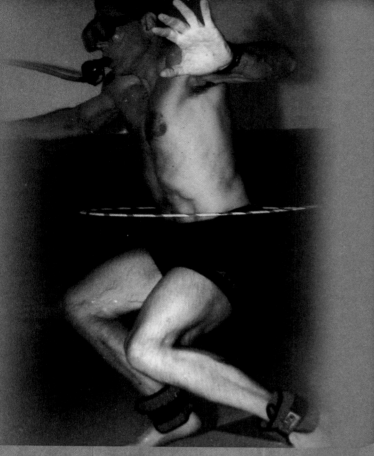

Photo: Guinness World Records Limited

Ashrita Furman (USA) Hula-Hooped under water for 2 minutes 38 seconds at an aquatic center in East Meadow, New York, on August 1, 2007.

Did You Know?

In four months in 1958, Wham-O sold 25 million of the first Hula-Hoop toy hoops for $1.98 each.

ACTIVITIES

1. Look around. How many things can you find that are shaped like a Hula-Hoop? List them.

   _____

   _____

2. With a friend, see who can keep a Hula-Hoop going the longest without letting it fall. How long did the winner keep going?

   _____

Longest Time Holding a Vertical Person Overhead

Photo: Guinness World Records Limited

On March 11, 2010, Markus Ferber (Germany) held Clarissa Beyelschmidt (Germany) in a standing position above his head for 1 minute 16.38 seconds.

Did You Know?

Legend has it that Milo of Croton, a sixth-century Greek wrestler, carried an ox across his shoulders through the Olympic stadium.

ACTIVITIES

1. The word *vertical* means "straight up and down." Use these vertical lines to draw a picture.

2. Twelve cheerleaders were held above their partners' heads for 30 seconds each. What is the total number of minutes the cheerleaders were held in the air?

Most Flexible Man

Photo: Guinness World Records Limited

Daniel Browning Smith (USA) is also known as "Rubber Boy." He can contort himself to fit into a box that is 13.5 in. (34.2 cm) long, 16 in. (40.6 cm) wide, and 19.5 in. (49.5 cm) high.

Did You Know?
Daniel Browning Smith can squeeze his body through a tennis racket in just 15 seconds!

ACTIVITIES

1. Using your body, form alphabet letters. Can a friend guess each letter?

   _____

2. How flexible are you? Can you touch your toes without bending your knees? Circle your answer.

   yes   **no**

3. When three rubber bands are stretched out, they are 8.5 inches, 12 inches, and 18 inches long. What is the difference between the longest and the shortest?

   _____

Stretchiest Skin

Photo: Guinness World Records Limited

On October 29, 1999, Garry Turner (UK) stretched the skin of his stomach to a distended length of 6.25 in. (15.8 cm) in Los Angeles, California.

Did You Know?

If you peeled off your skin, it would stretch to about 22 sq. ft. (2 m²) or the size of a picnic table.

CHECK THIS OUT!

Garry Turner (United Kingdom) has stretchy skin. In fact, he has the Stretchiest Skin on record.

There is a reason why Turner's skin is so stretchy. He has a rare condition called *Ehlers-Danlos Syndrome*, or EDS. In most human bodies, a protein called *collagen* holds cells together. You can think of it as glue for your body. People with EDS have faulty collagen that does not bind cells tightly to each other. That makes their skin very, very loose.

Turner has learned to live with EDS. Actually, he makes his living with it. He tours with a circus. People are amazed by his loose skin, and Turner says he loves making people smile.

1. List four things people use to bind things together when making or repairing things.

_____   _____

_____   _____

2. What does *bind* mean? Circle the best definition.

   a. to break apart

   b. to make curved or crooked

   c. to tangle up

   d. to fasten or hold together

3. Hold a ballpoint pen straight out from your stomach—that is about how far out Turner can pull his skin. How many inches is that? Mark it on the ruler.

4. Look around your home. List four things you find that stretch. What is the stretchiest thing you found? Circle it.

_____   _____

_____   _____

5. Draw a picture showing what you think you would look like with stretchy skin.

Fastest Time to Husk a Coconut

Photo: Guinness World Records Limited

On March 30, 2003, Sidaraju S. Raju (India) husked a 10-lb. 6.4-oz. (4.744 kg) coconut using his teeth in 28.06 seconds at the Ravindra Kalashetra, Bangalore, India.

Did You Know?

A drink, food, fuel, utensils, musical instruments, and more can be made from coconuts.

ACTIVITIES

1. A coconut is a fruit. How many fruits can you name?

_____   _____   _____

_____   _____   _____

_____   _____   _____

2. How fast can you peel an orange? Write your time in seconds.

_____

Heaviest Vehicle Pulled 100 Feet (Male)

Photo: Guinness World Records Limited

On September 15, 2008, Kevin Fast (Canada) pulled a 126,200 lb. (57,243 kg) fire truck for a distance of 100 ft. (30.48 m) in New York City, New York.

Did You Know?
Dalmatians used to ride with horse-drawn fire trucks to fires to protect the horses from horse thieves.

ACTIVITIES

1. A fire department has ladders that are 25 feet, 40 feet, and 72 feet long. Which ladder would be best used to reach a window 36 feet above the ground?

   _____

2. Three kinds of fire trucks are *pumper trucks*, *ladder trucks*, and *tanker trucks*. Tanker trucks can hold 1,000 gallons of water. If a tanker truck is $\frac{1}{3}$ full, how much water does it carry?

   _____

Heaviest Car Balanced on the Head

Photo: Guinness World Records Limited

On May 24, 1999, John Evans (UK) balanced a 352 lb. (159.6 kg) car on his head for 33 seconds at The London Studios, London, England.

Did You Know?
Evans's neck is a whopping 24 in. (60.96 cm) thick.

ACTIVITIES

1. Imagine you began balancing a book on your head at 1:00. You kept it balanced for 14 minutes before it dropped. Draw hands on the clock to show what time the book dropped.

2. Find a small, non-breakable object. Can you balance it on your head for 33 seconds? Circle your answer.

yes   no

Fastest Time to Burst Three Balloons With the Back

Photo: Guinness World Records Limited

On November 23, 2007, Julia Gunthel (Germany) popped three balloons with her back in 12 seconds on the set of *Guinness World Records–Die Größten Weltrekorde* in Cologne, Germany.

Did You Know?
The first balloons were made from animal stomachs, bladders, and intestines.

ACTIVITIES

Create an acrostic poem. Write a word that begins with each letter below.

b _____

a _____

l _____

l _____

o _____

o _____

n _____

Most Eggs Held in the Hand

Photo: Guinness World Records Limited

On March 21, 2009, Zachery George (USA) was able to hold 24 eggs in one of his hands.

Did You Know?
The larger a hen gets, the larger her eggs are.

CHECK THIS OUT!

When Zachery George (United States) was in school, he wanted to be the tallest man in the world. That wish did not come true, but George still wanted to break a world record. On March 21, 2009, he did. George broke the record for the Most Eggs Held in the Hand. He put 24 eggs in one hand and held them for 40 seconds. He beat the old record of 20 eggs held for 10 seconds.

He's not the only handy world record holder. On June 14, 2008, Rohit Timilsina (Nepal) held 21 tennis balls in one hand for 14.32 seconds. On September 19, 2011, Stephen Kish (United Kingdom) held 42 AA batteries in his hand, breaking the old record of 30 AA batteries.

1. If eggs cost $1.50 for each dozen, how much did George pay for the eggs he used?

   a. $1.50

   b. $3.50

   c. $3.00

   d. $4.50

2. How many more eggs did George hold than the old record holder?

   _____

3. One chicken egg weighs about two ounces. One pound is 16 ounces. About how many pounds of eggs did George hold in one hand?

   _____

4. Find small things such as crayons, marbles, or pieces of candy. How many can you hold in your hand at one time?

   _____

5. Tell these chicken and egg jokes to your friends.

Which side of a chicken has more feathers?

The outside!

Why did the hen cross the road?

To prove she wasn't chicken.

What do you get when a pig and a chicken bump into each other?

Ham and eggs!

How does a chicken tell time?

One o'cluck, two o'cluck, three o'cluck . . .

Tallest Boy

Photo: Guinness World Records Limited

Brenden Adams (USA) is 7 ft. 4.6 in. (225.1 cm) tall.

Did You Know?
Adams was the size of a three-year-old child when he was only 12 months old.

ACTIVITIES

1. List four things that are taller than you.

_____   _____

_____   _____

2. Who is the tallest person you know? Find out how tall that person is.

_____

3. Can you find a growth chart or baby book that tells your height at different ages? How tall were you at age two? Age six? How tall are you now?

_____

Shortest Stuntman

Photo: Guinness World Records Limited

On October 20, 2003, Kiran Shah (UK) measured 4 ft. 1.7 in. (1.26 m) tall. He has appeared in 52 movies since 1976.

Did You Know?

You can take classes to learn stunt work. They can teach you wire flying, unarmed combat, fire burns, and how to fall down stairs.

ACTIVITIES

1. Stand next to three friends or family members. Who is shortest? Who is tallest?

   _____

2. An action movie is 2 hours, 36 minutes long. If you begin watching it at 12:15, what time will it be when the movie is over?

   _____

3. The shortest stuntman is about 4 feet, 2 inches tall. The tallest boy (page 42) is about 7 feet, 5 inches tall. Give the difference.

   _____

Longest Beard (Living Person, Female)

Photo: Guinness World Records Limited

Vivian Wheeler (USA) began growing a full beard in 1990. The longest strand of hair measured 11 in. (27.9 cm) in 2000.

Did You Know?
Every day, 50 to 100 hairs fall out of your head, although new ones constantly grow in.

ACTIVITIES

1. Each day, about 75 hairs fall out of your head. Multiply 75 by the number of people in your family to find out how many hairs are lost at your house every day.

2. Draw a funny moustache and beard on this person.

Most Pirouettes on Pointe on the Head

Photo: Guinness World Records Limited

On December 21, 2006, Wu Zhengdan (China) completed three pirouettes on pointe while standing on the head of her husband, Wei Baohua (China), in Beijing, China.

Did You Know?

In the Pagoda bowl balance, a female acrobat balances a bowl of rice on her head while doing a handstand on another acrobat's head!

ACTIVITIES

1. Stand on one foot. How long can you hold your balance?

   _____

2. Spin around three times. What is something else you can spin?

   _____

3. Create a dance routine with a friend. Practice, then put on a show! How many people saw your show?

   _____

Longest Fingernails on a Female (Ever)

Photo: Guinness World Records Limited

On February 23, 2008, Lee Redmond's (USA) nails were 28 ft. 4.5 in. (8.65 m) long. She started to grow her nails in 1979.

Did You Know?
Fingernails grow four times faster than toenails.

CHECK THIS OUT!

In 1979, Lee Redmond (United States) decided to stop cutting her fingernails. For 30 years, she let them grow. By 2008, her nails had grown to a record length.

It must have been hard to have such long nails, but Redmond did not mind. She took good care of her nails, soaking them in olive oil every day and cleaning them with a toothbrush. Redmond's nails made her famous. Once, a TV show offered her $100,000 to cut her nails on live TV. She said no.

On February 11, 2009, Redmond was injured in a car accident. All of her nails broke off in the accident, but she knew she was lucky to be alive. "There really is more to me than my fingernails," she said.

1. Think about how you use your hands every day. What two things do you think would be hardest to do with very long fingernails?

_____

_____

2. What two things could long fingernails help you do?

_____

_____

3. Your fingertips are very sensitive. That's why you have fingernails to protect them. Have a friend put something in a bag. Touch it with your fingers. Don't look! Can you tell what it is? Take turns. Fill in the chart as you play the game.

What's in the bag?	Did I guess it?	Did a friend guess it?

4. Redmond started to grow her nails in 1979. How many years ago was that?

_____

5. Do you think you would want to try to break Redmond's record? Explain why or why not.

_____

_____

_____

Most Pierced Man

Photo: Guinness World Records Limited

As of October 17, 2008, John Lynch (UK) had 241 body piercings, including 151 in his head and neck.

Did You Know?

In ancient Egypt, only the pharaoh could have his navel pierced. Others might be executed.

ACTIVITIES

1. About how many piercings would Lynch have with 2.5 times as many? Round your answer to the nearest whole number.

2. People in ancient Egypt may have been the first to use body piercings. The scarab beetle was a symbol used in Egyptian jewelry. Decorate this scarab beetle.

Most Eggs Crushed With the Wrist in 30 Seconds

Photo: Guinness World Records Limited

On September 20, 2005, Balakrishnan Sivasamy (Malaysia) successfully crushed 25 eggs with his wrist in 30 seconds at a restaurant in Perak, Malaysia.

Did You Know?

The measurement of your arm, from your elbow to your wrist, is the same as the length of your foot. Check it out!

ACTIVITIES

1. Make a fun goal, like catching 20 balls or blowing up three balloons. Can you reach your goal in 30 seconds? Write what you did.

   _____

2. The word *egg* has a double consonant, *gg*. List other words you know that have a double consonant.

   _____ _____ _____

   _____ _____ _____

Fastest Time to Enter a Suitcase

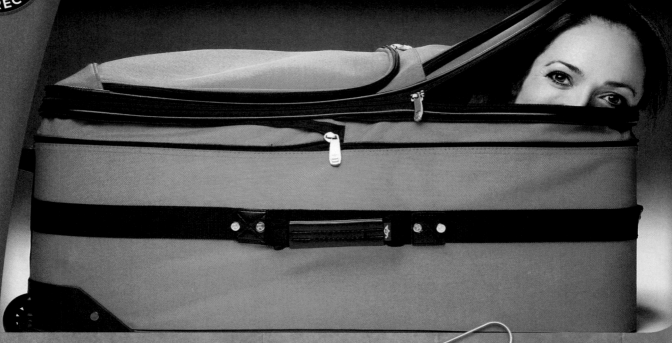

Photo: Guinness World Records Limited

On September 14, 2009, Leslie Tipton (USA) successfully entered a zippered suitcase in 5.43 seconds in New York City, New York, as part of the *Guinness World Records 2010* launch.

Did You Know?

If you are double-jointed, you can probably bend your thumb backwards until it touches your wrist.

ACTIVITIES

1. Imagine you are taking a trip to New York City. List what you will pack in your suitcase.

   _____   _____   _____

   _____   _____   _____

2. Play a speedy game of hide-and-seek. Allow only five seconds to find a hiding place. Write the best hiding place you found.

   _____

Most People Fire Breathing

Photo: Guinness World Records Limited

On April 23, 2009, in Maastricht, Netherlands, 293 people breathed fire at the same time.

Did You Know?
October 9 is Fire Prevention Day, marking the date when Mrs. O'Leary's cow kicked over a lamp that started the Great Chicago Fire.

ACTIVITIES

1. To set this record, 293 people breathed fire. How many more people did this group need to reach 350?

   _____

2. Write one way you can help prevent a fire at your home.

   _____

3. Does your family have a place to meet outside in case of a fire? Write where you will meet.

   _____

Longest Ear Hair

Photo: Guinness World Records Limited

Anthony Victor (India) has hair sprouting from the center of his outer ears that measures 7.12 in. (18.1 cm) at its longest point.

Did You Know?

The ear bones (malleus, incus, and stapes) are the smallest bones in the human body and could fit on a penny.

CHECK THIS OUT!

Humans are mammals. We have hair all over our bodies. The hair on our heads is the most noticeable. It grows about 0.5 inches each month. Some people let their hair grow really long.

Anthony Victor (India) lets his hair grow long, too. However, the hair is not on top of his head. His record-breaking hair grows around the rims of his ears!

Toshie Kawakami (Japan) also lets his hair grow long, but in his case, that hair is on his eyebrows! On June 30, 2011, his longest eyebrow hair measured in at 7.01 in.

Complete the statements by writing words you read on page 52. Then look in the puzzle to find the words you wrote. Search across and down.

Humans and other living things that have hair are _____.

Three bones inside the human ear are the _____, the

_____, and the _____.

The record holder for the longest ear hair is Anthony _____.

The most noticeable hair on humans is the hair on our _____.

Anthony Victor has hair sprouting from the center of his outer _____.

Victor is from the country of _____.

Victor's ear hair is about _____ inches long.

Toshi _____ also has unusually long hair on his face.

Kawakami's _____ are about seven inches long.

Kawakami is from the country of _____.

m	a	l	l	e	u	s	s	t
i	n	d	i	a	j	s	t	m
i	n	c	u	s	a	e	a	a
e	a	r	s	s	p	v	p	m
w	d	s	r	e	a	e	e	m
h	e	a	d	s	n	n	s	a
v	i	c	t	o	r	i	i	l
k	a	w	a	k	a	m	i	s
e	y	e	b	r	o	w	s	n

Most Powerful Lungs

Photo: Guinness World Records Limited

On September 16, 1998, Manjit Singh (UK) blew up a meteorological balloon to a diameter of 8 ft. (2.44 m) in 42 minutes at the Rushley Pavilion Centre, Leicester, United Kingdom.

Did You Know?

A sneeze travels 100 mph (160 km/h), and a cough travels 60 mph (97 km/h).

ACTIVITIES

1. Put a dollar bill against a wall. Using only your breath (no hands), how long can you keep the dollar bill up?

   _____

2. How fast can you blow up a balloon? Ask a friend to time you.

   _____

3. A meteorological balloon gives weather information. Look outside. Draw a picture of the weather today.

Longest Fingernails on a Male (Ever)

On May 30, 2009, Melvin Boothe's (USA) fingernails were a combined length of 32 ft. 3.8 in. (9.85 m).

Photo: Guinness World Records Limited

Did You Know?

Another record holder, Shridhar Chillal (India), has not cut his fingernails since 1952. They are so long his wife gets up each night to turn him over.

ACTIVITIES

1. If the combined length of Boothe's 10 fingernails is 32 feet, what is the combined length of his fingernails on just one hand?

   _____

2. Fingernails grow four times as fast as toenails. If you trim your fingernails every week, how many times will you need to trim your toenails in one month?

   _____

Longest Beard Dreadlock (Living Male)

Photo: Guinness World Records Limited

On November 23, 2008, Shri Shri Baba Shri Ji's (India) beard measured 6 ft. (1.84 m) from the end of his chin to the tip of the beard.

Did You Know?
Hair can grow into dreadlocks if it is not combed for three to six months.

ACTIVITIES

1. What amazing things could you do if you had very, very long hair? Write your ideas.

_____

_____

2. The record holder's beard is six feet long. That's 72 inches! Write the difference in inches between the record-breaking beard and your height.

_____

Tallest Married Couple (Living)

Photo: Guinness World Records Limited

Wilco (Netherlands) and Keisha van Kleef-Bolton (UK) have a combined average height of 13 ft. 3.3 in. (4.047 m). Wilco is 6 ft. 9.75 in. (2.076 m) tall and Keisha is 6 ft. 5.5 in. (1.968 m) tall.

Did You Know?
Wilco and Keisha have children who are already the tallest in their classes!

ACTIVITIES

1. Two are taller than one! Working with a friend, measure your heights. What is the total of your height and your friend's height?

_____

2. The average doorway is about 80 inches tall. If one person had the height of you and your friend combined (answer #1), could that person fit through a doorway? Circle your answer.

yes   **no**

Longest Tongue

Stephen Taylor's (UK) tongue measured 3.86 in. (9.8 cm) long from the tip to his closed upper lip on February 11, 2009.

Photo: Guinness World Records Limited

Did You Know?
Your tongue moves saliva around even when you're sleeping, or you would drool all over your pillow!

CHECK THIS OUT!

Your tongue is a very important part of your body. You need your tongue to chew, swallow, talk, and taste.

Now, stick out your tongue! When Stephen Taylor (United Kingdom) did, Guinness World Records judges found that he had the world's Longest Tongue. They measured from the tip of Taylor's tongue to his closed top lip. The part that stuck out was 3.86 inches long.

Chanel Tapper (United States) has a long tongue, too. Her tongue measured 3.8 inches. These tongue lengths do not include the part that is still in the mouth. The average length of the whole human tongue is four inches. Taylor and Tapper won records with just the tips of their tongues!

1. Draw a line above the ruler to show the length of Taylor's tongue.

2. Stick out your tongue. Ask a friend to measure it from the tip to your closed top lip. Draw a line above the ruler to show the length of your tongue.

3. Use your answer to #2. How much longer would your tongue need to grow to set the record for the world's Longest Tongue?

_____

4. The taste buds on your tongue detect four kinds of flavors. Write a favorite food for each flavor type.

Sweet: _____

Sour: _____

Bitter: _____

Salty: _____

5. Your nose and tongue work together to taste foods. Try smelling a slice of onion while taking a bite of something else, such as an apple. What do you taste?

_____

_____

Heaviest Weight Lifted With One Ear

Photo: Guinness World Records Limited

On January 3, 2009, Zafar Gill (Pakistan) lifted 160 lb. 15 oz. (73 kg) gym weights that were clamped to his ear.

Did You Know?
You do not use your ear muscles to wiggle them—you use muscles in your scalp!

ACTIVITIES

1. Eating nutritious food builds muscle strength. Circle your favorite healthy foods.

salad	yogurt	turkey
carrots	cheese	eggs
apples	beans	cherries

2. Your ears are amazing! Make a noise with a toy or another object. Can your friend in the next room guess what made the sound? Take turns. What sound was hardest to guess?

Most Consecutive Foot-Juggling Flips

Photo: Guinness World Records Limited

Hou Yanan (China) juggled Jiang Tiantian (China) with her feet for 90 consecutive flips in Beijing, China, on September 19, 2007.

Did You Know?
Some scientists believe that juggling can increase your brainpower!

ACTIVITIES

1. How long is a foot? It's about the same length as an average man's foot—12 inches! How long is your foot?

   _____

2. Make a footbag by filling a balloon with sand or dried beans and tying it shut. Then, play hacky sack with a friend. Keep the footbag off the ground without using your hands. How many passes can you make before the footbag drops?

   _____

Largest Tonsils

Justin Dodge (USA) had tonsils that measured 1.3 in. (3.2 cm) long, 1 in. (2.6 cm) wide, and 0.8 in. (2.1 cm) thick. They were surgically removed on December 18, 2008.

Did You Know?
Most six-year-old children's tonsils are larger than their parents' tonsils!

Photo: Guinness World Records Limited

ACTIVITIES

Your tonsils can swell when you have a cold. Write letters to complete ways to take care of yourself when you are sick. Finish the sentence by writing the word formed by the circled letters.

d (___) ___nk flui___s

co___(e)___ you___ mou___ ___

vi (s) i ___ the do___to___

ea (___) hea___th___ f___ ___ds

Most important: Get plenty of _____!

Heaviest Weight Pulled With the Eye Sockets

Photo: Guinness World Records Limited

On April 25, 2009, Chayne "The Space Cowboy" Hultgren (Australia) successfully pulled 907 lb. (411.65 kg) in Milan, Italy, using his eye sockets.

Did You Know?
Your eyes blink more than 4 million times a year!

ACTIVITIES

1. Did you know you blink 12 times per minute? How many times do you blink in 30 minutes?

   _____

2. How many times do you blink in one hour?

   _____

3. We say that something very quick happens "in the blink of an eye." What can you do "in the blink of an eye"?

   _____

Loudest Scream

Photo: Guinness World Records Limited

Classroom assistant Jill Drake (UK) had a scream that reached 129 decibels when measured at the Halloween festivities held in the Millennium Dome, London, United Kingdom, in October 2000.

Did You Know?
A frightened pig screams just about as loud as the scream of a jet engine taking off.

ACTIVITIES

1. Write about something that made you scream.

_____

_____

2. Close your eyes. What's the softest sound you hear?

_____

3. Keep your eyes closed. What's the loudest sound you hear?

_____

Photo: Guinness World Records Limited

FANTASTIC RECORDS

Photo: Guinness World Records Limited

Farthest Distance Limbo Skating Under Cars

Photo: Guinness World Records Limited

The farthest distance limbo skating under cars is 126 ft. 11 in. (38.68 m) and was achieved by Rohan Ajit Kokane (India) on February 17, 2011.

Did You Know?
Kokane skated under 20 cars.

ACTIVITIES

1. Turn on some music. Find a broom handle and use it to play limbo with two friends. Who got the lowest?

_____

2. The record holder skated under 20 cars. What is $\frac{1}{4}$ of 20?

_____

3. Which do you think is easier: roller skating or riding a bicycle? Explain why.

_____

_____

Most Hugs Given in One Hour by an Individual

Photo: Guinness World Records Limited

Nick Vujicic (USA) gave 1,749 hugs in one hour on September 25, 2010, at the Deschutes County Expo Center in Oregon.

Did You Know?
Vujicic, a quadriplegic, hugged all sorts of people young and old, including disabled people and those with special needs.

ACTIVITIES

1. Hugs are good for you! They provide comfort and can even lower your blood pressure. Who did you hug today?

   _____

2. Vujicic gave 1,749 hugs. How many more hugs would make the total 2,500?

   _____

3. Setting this record took one hour. What will you spend one hour doing tomorrow?

   _____

Photo: Guinness World Records Limited

Paula Mairer (Austria) ran a half marathon backward in a time of 2 hours 49 minutes 48 seconds on October 10, 2004.

Did You Know?

Abebe Bikila (Ethiopia) broke a world marathon record once with bare feet (in 1960) and once with shoes (in 1964).

ACTIVITIES

1. A marathon is a race 26.2 miles long. What place is about 26 miles away from your home? Use a map or ask an adult.

   _____

2. If a marathon is about 26 miles, a half marathon is about how long?

   _____

3. Run a short race while a friend times you. Run it again backward. Which time was faster?

   _____

Most Heads Shaved in One Hour

Photo: Guinness World Records Limited

Barber John McGuire (Ireland) shaved 60 heads in one hour in Dublin, Ireland, on February 18, 2010. He did it to help raise money for charity.

Did You Know?

In ancient Greece, boys cut their hair short when they became teenagers.

ACTIVITIES

1. Sixty heads were shaved in one hour. How many heads could the barber shave in 24 hours?

   _____

2. Draw a silly hairstyle on this head.

Most Pumpkins Carved in One Hour

Photo: Guinness World Records Limited

On October 7, 2010, David Finkle (UK) carved 102 pumpkins in one hour in Essex, United Kingdom.

Did You Know?

The tradition of pumpkin carving began not with pumpkins, but with turnips, beets, and potatoes instead.

CHECK THIS OUT!

Many people carve pumpkins in the fall for seasonal decorations, but not many people set world records while doing it!

Before David Finkle's (United Kingdom) world record attempt, 70 pumpkins were prepared for him to begin carving when the clock started ticking.

However, in just 20 minutes, Finkle had already carved 40 pumpkins! So, he decided to go even further and try for 100 pumpkins in one hour. The crew and his family then hollowed out more pumpkins as he worked so that he could continue without stopping. Finkle stopped carving after 59 minutes when he was certain that he'd carved over 100 pumpkins.

ACTIVITIES

1. Finkle carved 40 pumpkins after 20 minutes. How many pumpkins did he carve per minute?

   _____

2. The world's Heaviest Pumpkin weighed about 1,810 pounds. If an average pumpkin weighs 10 pounds, how many average pumpkins would it take to weigh the same as the Heaviest Pumpkin?

   _____

3. During his world record attempt, Finkle beat his original goal of carving 70 pumpkins and pushed himself to go further. Write about a time when you accomplished a goal and then pushed yourself to achieve even more. How did it make you feel?

   _____

   _____

   _____

4. Draw happy, silly, wacky, or scary faces on these pumpkins.

Fastest Time to Crawl One Mile

Photo: Guinness World Records Limited

The fastest time to crawl one mile (1.6 km) is 23 minutes 45 seconds and was set by Suresh Joachim (Canada) in Toronto, Ontario, Canada, in 2007.

Did You Know?

Some babies crawl forward on their hands and knees, but others crawl backward, scoot on their bottoms, or roll.

ACTIVITIES

1. Run a short race in different ways while a friend times you. Try running, crawling, jumping, and skipping. Which way of moving was the fastest?

   _____

2. The record holder crawled for one mile in about 23 minutes. Could he crawl for two miles in one hour? Circle your answer.

   yes   no

Longest Marathon on a Seesaw

Photo: Guinness World Records Limited

The longest time spent continuously on a seesaw was 75 hours 10 minutes. The record was set by Brandi Carbee and Natalie Svenvold (both USA) in September 2004 in Puyallup, Washington.

Did You Know?
At the Japanese playground *Nishi-Rokugo*, or Tire Park, kids play on bridges and slides made from over 3,000 tires.

ACTIVITIES

1. What are your favorite things to do at a park?

   _____   _____

2. The record holders stayed on the seesaw for about 75 hours. For about how many days did they seesaw?

   _____

3. It takes two people to seesaw or to play catch. What other activities are most fun with two people?

   _____

Fastest Mile Balancing a Soccer Ball on the Head

On March 20, 2010, Yee Ming Low (Malaysia) ran a mile in 8 minutes 35 seconds while balancing a soccer ball on his head.

Photo: Guinness World Records Limited

Did You Know?
In many cultures, people carry heavy loads on their heads. Children even carry stacks of school books that way.

ACTIVITIES

1. How many steps can you take while balancing a ball on your head?

_____

2. How many feet are in one mile? Use a reference book or a Web site to find the answer.

_____

3. What is your favorite sport to play with a ball?

_____

Longest Marbles Playing Marathon

Photo: Guinness World Records Limited

Michael Gray and Jenna Gray (both Australia) spent 26 hours playing marbles continuously. They played in Sydney, Australia, in 2006.

Did You Know?

Have you heard of "playing for keeps"? In marbles, if you play "keepsies," you can forfeit your marbles. If you play "friendlies," players take their own marbles home.

ACTIVITIES

1. Some people collect marbles. List things you collect.

   _____   _____

   _____   _____

2. The record holders played marbles for 26 hours. Is that more or less than one whole day? Circle your answer.

   more than one day   **less than one day**

3. Marbles are made from glass. What else is made from glass?

   _____

Fastest Mile of Pennies

Photo: Guinness World Records Limited

The fastest time to lay down a mile of pennies is 2 hours 16 minutes 9 seconds and was achieved by the Burnt Hickory Youth Ministry (USA) in Marietta, Georgia, on August 2, 2008.

Did You Know?
The average penny lasts 25 years.

CHECK THIS OUT!

Pennies may seem like small objects, but on August 2, 2008, Burnt Hickory Youth Ministry (United States) used them to set a big record!

The group achieved the world record for laying down a mile of pennies in the fastest time. The event raised over $16,000 for humanitarian aid for Honduras. It is estimated that nearly 85,000 pennies were needed to complete the mile.

Pennies were the very first coins ever created in the United States. The U.S. Mint has been making pennies since 1793, and each year, it produces more than 13 billion pennies. On average, about 30 million pennies a day are produced—that's 1,040 pennies every second!

1. A penny is $\frac{3}{4}$ of an inch wide. It would take 16 pennies to form one foot. There are 5,280 feet in a mile. How many pennies would it take to form one mile?

_____

2. Find Honduras on a map. What continent is it on? Is it in the northern or southern hemisphere?

_____

3. If 85,000 pennies were used in setting this world record, how many dollars were used? Circle the answer.

   a. $8,500.00

   b. $850.00

   c. $8.50

   d. $85,000.00

4. Look for pennies around your home or school. Collect them all for one week. How many did you find?

_____

5. Toss a penny and catch it in the palm of your hand 10 times. Fill in the chart to show your results.

Toss	1	2	3	4	5	6	7	8	9	10
Heads or Tails?										

6. Flip the coin one more time. Predict whether it will land on heads or tails. Was your prediction correct?

_____

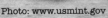
Photo: www.usmint.gov

Fastest Three-Legged Half Marathon

WORLD
@ RECORD
ATTEMPT

Photo: Guinness World Records Limited

The record for the fastest time to complete a three-legged half marathon is held by Alastair and Nick Benbow (both UK). They ran the London half marathon in 1 hour 37 minutes 53 seconds on March 2, 2003.

Did You Know?
The record holders were also tied together at the wrist.

ACTIVITIES

1. Set up a three-legged race for friends. Mark a start and finish line. Use scarves to tie pairs together loosely at the ankle. Who won?

_____

2. After the three-legged race, stay tied together at the ankle with a friend for part of the day. What activities were hardest to do while you were three-legged?

_____

Fastest One Mile Piggy Back Race

Photo: Guinness World Records Limited

Ashrita Furman carried Bipin Larkin (both USA) piggy back for one mile (1.61 km) in 12 minutes 47 seconds on July 4, 2010, in New York City, New York.

Did You Know?

A space satellite loaded for transport is said to be "piggy backed" on the launcher.

ACTIVITIES

1. Do you remember a time when you were very small and an adult carried you piggy back? Write about it.

_____

_____

2. The record was set in about 12 minutes. What goal can you reach in 12 minutes? Can you do 100 math problems correctly or take a shower? Write what you did.

_____

Fastest Mile Balancing a Baseball Bat on a Finger

Photo: Guinness World Records Limited

Ashrita Furman (USA) ran one mile while balancing a baseball bat on his finger in 7 minutes 5 seconds on June 20, 2009, in Queens, New York.

Did You Know?

Most amateur players use aluminum bats, but pros use wood. One reason is that fans like to hear the "crack" of a hit with a wood bat.

ACTIVITIES

1. Practice balancing different objects on one finger. Try a pencil or a spoon. Write what you did.

   _____

2. About how many times could Furman run the race in one hour? Round your answer to the nearest whole number.

   _____

3. A baseball runner crosses first, second, third, and home plate to score. How many plates would be crossed for eight runs?

   _____

Most Skips on a Unicycle in One Minute

Photo: Guinness World Records Limited

Daiki Izumida, also known as *Shiojyari* (Japan), skipped rope while on his unicycle 214 times in one minute in Hong Kong, China, on August 12, 2007.

Did You Know?

Engineers are studying how unicycles work to help invent new one-wheeled personal mobility devices.

ACTIVITIES

1. How many times can you skip rope in one minute?

   _____

2. The record holder skipped 214 times in one minute. How many times could he skip in 15 minutes?

   _____

3. The word part *uni* means "one." Write *uni* on the lines to make words.

   _____cycle   _____verse

   _____corn   _____son

Most Consecutive Double Dutch Style Skips (Team)

Photo: Guinness World Records Limited

The most consecutive Double Dutch style skips by a team are 371 and were achieved by the Summerwind Skippers (USA) in Boise, Idaho, on November 11, 2010.

Did You Know?
Early jump ropes were made of vines found in jungles.

CHECK THIS OUT!

The Summerwind Skippers, a performance and competitive jump rope sports team, are very dedicated to their sport. They were able to prove just how dedicated they are when five high school students set the world record for most consecutive Double Dutch style skips. Double Dutch style means you jump with two ropes instead of just one.

Children have been jumping rope since the Middle Ages, or even earlier! Jumping rope is good, fun exercise to do by yourself or with friends. When you jump rope, you are strengthening the muscles in your legs and upper arms, increasing the flow of blood through your body, and speeding up your heart rate. This means you're getting an aerobic workout.

ACTIVITIES

Complete the crossword puzzle with words you read on page 82.

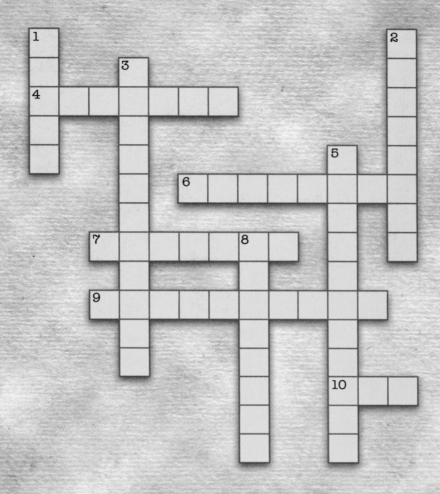

Across

4. Jump roping gives your body an ____ workout.

6. All the equipment you need to get some exercise and have fun

7. Jumping rope strengthens the ____ in your legs and arms.

9. Children have been jumping rope since this time in history.

10. Double Dutch requires ____ jump ropes.

Down

1. State where the Summerwind Skippers set their record

2. The record holders are the Double Dutch Summerwind ____.

3. The Summerwind Skippers hold the record for the Most ____ Double Dutch Style Skips.

5. Sport that uses two jump ropes

8. Double Dutch skipping is a great way to get this.

Most Cartwheels in One Minute

Photo: Guinness World Records Limited

Ten-year-old Yash Kumar B. Patel (India) completed 63 cartwheels in one minute on the TV set of *Guinness World Records* in Mumbai, India, on March 15, 2011.

Did You Know?
In an aerial cartwheel, the gymnast's hands never touch the ground.

ACTIVITIES

1. Is there a skill you can do 63 times, such as skipping rope or dribbling a ball? Try it. Write what you did.

   _____

2. Sixty-three cartwheels were done in one minute. How many cartwheels could be done in five minutes?

   _____

3. Do your friends have special talents? Gather performers for an "amazing feats" video or live show. Name your show.

   _____

Most Consecutive Chin-Ups

Photo: Guinness World Records Limited

At age 70, Lee Chin-Yong (Korea) did 612 consecutive chin-ups. He completed them in 2 hours 40 minutes in Seoul, South Korea, on December 29, 1994.

Did You Know?

Taekwondo, a martial art, is one of the most popular activities in Korea. Its name means "art of the hand and foot."

ACTIVITIES

1. The record holder did 612 chin-ups. What is $\frac{1}{3}$ of 612?

_____

2. What does the saying "keep your chin up" mean?

_____

3. What is your favorite way to play and exercise using the muscles in your arms?

_____

Greatest Grape-Catching Distance

Photo: Guinness World Records Limited

The greatest distance at which a grape thrown from ground level was caught in the mouth was 354 ft. 4 in. (108 m). The grape catcher was Paul E. Lyday III (USA), who achieved the record in Fort Motte, South Carolina, in 2009.

Did You Know?
The grape was launched from a pouch attached to two elastic bands.

ACTIVITIES

1. Catch a ball thrown by a friend. Back up about a foot and catch it again. Keep backing up. About how many feet was your longest catch?

_____

2. Grapes are fruits. List fruits you would like to eat in a fruit salad.

_____   _____   _____

_____   _____   _____

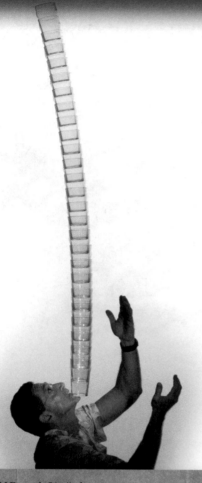

Photo: Guinness World Records Limited

Ashrita Furman (USA) balanced 81 drinking glasses (20 oz. size) on his chin for 12.10 seconds in Jamaica, New York, in 2007.

Did You Know?

If you have good balance, thank your cerebellum. That part of the brain at the back of the head controls movement and coordination.

ACTIVITIES

1. The record holder balanced 81 drinking glasses. What is the square root of 81?

   _____

2. Drinking water is important, especially when you exercise. How many glasses of water did you drink today?

   _____

3. What small, unbreakable object can you balance on your chin?

   _____

Fastest Time to Pop 1,000 Balloons

Photo: Guinness World Records Limited

The record for the fastest time to pop 1,000 balloons is 8.78 seconds and was achieved by OC&C Strategy Consultants (UK) in Barcelona, Spain, on September 8, 2007.

Did You Know?

A 100-foot-diameter balloon can lift 33,000 pounds.

CHECK THIS OUT!

Popping balloons is a fun way to burst into the record books! On September 8, 2007, the OC&C Strategy Consultants (United Kingdom) set the world record by popping 1,000 balloons in less than nine seconds. But they weren't the only ones to try their hand at balloon-popping.

The world record for the Fastest Time to Pop 100 Balloons by a Dog belongs to Anastasia, owned by Doree Sitterly (United States). The Jack Russell terrier popped 100 balloons in 44.49 seconds, breaking her own record on live television. Sitterly discovered Anastasia's hidden talent one year at a New Year's Eve party. When balloons came out to celebrate the new year, Anastasia went crazy over them!

1. One thousand balloons were popped in about nine seconds. At this rate, about how many could be popped in one minute? Use a calculator to help you.

_____

2. Anastasia popped 100 balloons in 44.49 seconds. About how long would it take her to pop 1,000 balloons?

_____

3. Put a balloon between your knees. How many steps can you take without popping it?

_____

4. Volley a balloon back and forth with a friend. For how many seconds can you keep it in the air?

_____

5. If you received five balloons every year on your birthday, how many would you have received by now?

_____

Fastest 10 Meters Balancing a Cue Stick on the Chin

Photo: Guinness World Records Limited

Ashrita Furman (USA) balanced a cue stick on his chin while running for 10 meters (32.8 ft.) in 3.02 seconds in Jamaica, New York, on August 30, 2009.

Did You Know?
The game of pool, or billiards, was once played exclusively by kings and other royals.

ACTIVITIES

1. Pool is played with seven solid colored balls, seven striped balls, and one black ball. How many balls are there in all?

_____

2. To begin the game, pool balls are placed in a triangular rack. Draw pool balls in this rack.

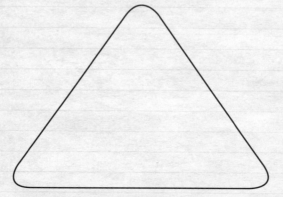

Most Balloons Inflated by the Nose in Three Minutes

Photo: Guinness World Records Limited

Andrew Dahl (USA) used his nose to inflate 23 balloons in three minutes on the set of a TV show in Rome, Italy, on March 18, 2010.

Did You Know?
A sneeze can send particles shooting out of your nose at 100 mph (161 km/h).

ACTIVITIES

1. Dahl inflated 23 balloons in three minutes. How many balloons could he inflate in nine minutes?

   _____

2. How many seconds does it take you to pop three balloons?

   _____

3. Write what you would do with 23 balloons.

   _____

Most Push-Ups in 12 Hours

Paddy Doyle (UK) completed 19,325 push-ups in 12 hours on May 1, 1989, in Birmingham, United Kingdom.

Photo: Guinness World Records Limited

Did You Know?
You have over 600 muscles. Some muscles can be controlled, but others (like your heart) are involuntary and work all by themselves.

ACTIVITIES

1. How many push-ups can you do?

_____

2. The record holder spent 12 hours doing push-ups. What have you spent 12 hours doing in the past week?

_____

3. At a rate of six push-ups per minute, how many push-ups could you do in 15 minutes?

_____

Fastest Mile Hula-Hooping While Balancing a Milk Bottle on the Head

Photo: Guinness World Records Limited

On December 7, 2007, Ashrita Furman (USA) ran a mile in 13 minutes 50 seconds while Hula-Hooping and balancing a milk bottle on his head in Punta Cana, Dominican Republic.

Did You Know?
Before 1950, most homes did not have reliable refrigerators to keep milk fresh. A "milk man" would deliver a bottle each day.

ACTIVITIES

1. The record is 13 minutes, 50 seconds. How many seconds faster would the runner have to be to make it 13 minutes, 12 seconds?

   _____

2. Hula-Hoop while chanting the ABCs. What letter did you get to before the hoop dropped?

   _____

3. What kind of smoothie do you like to make with milk?

   _____

Longest Duration Juggling Three Objects While Suspended

Photo: Guinness World Records Limited

The longest duration juggling three objects while suspended upside down by gravity boots is 6 minutes 46 seconds, achieved by Zdeněk Bradáč (Czech Republic), in Jablonec nad Nisou, Czech Republic, on November 1, 2010.

Did You Know?
Juggling has been around for about 4,000 years.

CHECK THIS OUT!

Juggling two balls can be difficult for some people, and juggling three balls can be even harder. But can you imagine juggling three balls while hanging upside down?

Zdeněk Bradáč (Czech Republic) set a record doing just that! The magician, juggler, and escapologist suspended himself to hang upside down with gravity boots. He then set a world record by juggling three balls for 6 minutes, 46 seconds and successfully catching them 1,276 times!

But Bradáč isn't the only one in the record books for juggling. On August 11, 2011, Niels Duinker (Netherlands) set a record for juggling three objects while blindfolded!

ACTIVITIES

1. During Bradáč's world record attempt, he successfully juggled three balls, catching them 1,276 times. What is $\frac{1}{4}$ of 1,276?

_____

2. Look at your answer to #1. Are you able to toss and catch a ball that many times? Circle your answer.

yes　　　　　　　　　**no**

3. Do you like to watch people juggling? Explain why or why not.

_____

_____

4. Find the Czech Republic and the Netherlands on a map. Are the two countries close to each other? Which country would you rather visit? Why?

_____

5. Learning to juggle takes time and practice. Read the steps below for juggling three balls. Number the steps in order from 1–5.

_____ Repeat steps 1–4.

_____ Hold two balls in your right hand and one ball in your left hand. Toss ball #1 from your right hand.

_____ As ball #2 reaches the top of the arc, toss ball #3 from your right hand up and underneath ball #2. Catch ball #2.

_____ Catch ball #3.

_____ As ball #1 reaches the top of the arc, toss ball #2 from your left hand up and under ball #1. Catch ball #1.

Longest Duration Balancing on One Foot

Photo: Guinness World Records Limited

Arulanantham Suresh Joachim (Sri Lanka) balanced on one foot for 76 hours 40 minutes in May 1997.

Did You Know?

Why do flamingos stand on one foot? It may be that keeping one foot out of the water helps them conserve body heat.

ACTIVITIES

1. How long can you balance on one foot? Have a friend time you.

_____

2. For about how many days did the record holder balance on one foot?

_____

3. What is the tree pose in yoga? Ask an adult or use a Web site to find out.

_____

Longest Distance Run While on Fire (Full-Body Burn Without Oxygen)

Photo: Guinness World Records Limited

In 2009, stunt man Keith Malcolm (UK) of The Stannage International Stunt Team ran 259 ft. (78.9 m) while on fire.

Did You Know?
The runner's clothes were doused in gasoline before being set on fire. The stunt was monitored by firefighters.

ACTIVITIES

1. Fire is a powerful force. It can be harmful and helpful. Write two ways fire can be harmful.

   _____   _____

2. Write two ways fire can be helpful.

   _____   _____

3. Write one way you and your family can help prevent fire.

   _____

Most Two-Finger (One-Arm) Push-Ups in One Minute

Photo: Guinness World Records Limited

Mohammed Mohammed Ali Zeinhom (Egypt) did 46 two-finger push-ups in one minute in front of the Giza Pyramids in Cairo, Egypt, on March 8, 2010.

Did You Know?
The push-ups were done using the pointer finger and thumb.

ACTIVITIES

1. Forty-six push-ups took one minute. About how many could be done in 15 seconds? Round to the nearest whole number.

   _____

2. Try brushing your teeth using only two fingers. Was it easy or difficult? Why?

   _____

   _____

Longest Basketball Dribbling Marathon

Lucknow Public Col
ndia : The country of Mind'

Photo: Guinness World Records Limited

In December 2007, Pawan Kumar Srivastava (India) dribbled a basketball for 55 hours 26 minutes in Lucknow, India.

Did You Know?
Originally, basketball was played with closed baskets. After a point was made, someone would climb a ladder to get the ball down.

ACTIVITIES

1. How many more minutes of dribbling would make the record 56 hours?

   _____

2. How many times can you dribble a ball without missing?

   _____

3. Circle your favorite part of playing basketball.

   running   **shooting**

   dribbling   **passing**

Most Grapes Caught by Mouth in One Minute

Photo: Guinness World Records Limited

Ashrita Furman (USA) caught 85 grapes by mouth in one minute in Jamaica, New York, on September 9, 2010.

Did You Know?
To crush grapes for wine making, people used to stomp on grapes in large vats with their bare feet.

CHECK THIS OUT!

For this record, Ashrita Furman (United States) caught 85 grapes in his mouth in one minute. Furman is no stranger to Guinness World Records. He has set 362 official Guinness Records, including the official record for Most Current Guinness World Records Held at the Same Time by an Individual. Furman first leaped into the record books in 1979 by doing 27,000 jumping jacks.

So what drives Furman to attempt these challenges? "I'm trying to show others that our human capacity is unlimited if we can truly believe in ourselves," he said. Furman says that each record he sets requires a great deal of determination, concentration, and fitness.

1. Write a sentence using the word *unlimited*.

_____

_____

2. Going at the same pace as he did during his world record attempt, how many grapes could Furman catch in his mouth in five minutes?

_____

3. Grapes are a healthy snack. Circle your favorite healthy snacks. Put a star beside the fruits.

banana	**cheese and wheat crackers**
yogurt	**cereal**
grapes	**carrot sticks**
peanut butter and celery	**apple slices**

4. Furman set his very first record by doing 27,000 jumping jacks. Count how many jumping jacks you can do before you get tired. Color in one star for each 10 jumping jacks you complete.

Longest Darts Playing Marathon (Singles)

Photo: Guinness World Records Limited

In November 2010, Paul O'Shaughnessy and Lenny McNevin (both Canada) played singles darts for 36 hours 10 minutes 10 seconds in Oshawa, Ontario, Canada.

Did You Know?
Colorful poison dart frogs are some of the most toxic animals on Earth. Their venom has been used to make poison arrows.

ACTIVITIES

1. In darts, each player needs three darts. How many darts would 15 players need?

   _____

2. Darts players stand about eight feet away from the board. Are most adults taller or shorter than eight feet? Circle your answer.

   shorter   **taller**

3. The center of a dartboard is called the *bull's-eye*. What does the saying "you hit the bull's-eye" usually mean?

   _____

Most Basketball Bounces in One Minute

Photo: Guinness World Records Limited

In 2010, Thaneswar Guragai (Nepal) bounced a basketball 444 times in one minute.

Did You Know?
Kangaroos can bounce six feet high and can cover 25 feet with a single leap.

ACTIVITIES

1. How many times can you bounce a ball in one minute? Ask a friend to time you.

   _____

2. List animals that bounce when they move.

   _____   _____

3. A ball was bounced 444 times in one minute. How many times could it be bounced in 90 seconds?

   _____

Longest Time in an Abdominal Plank Position

Photo: Guinness World Records Limited

At age 68, Paul Drinan (Australia) held an abdominal plank position for 33 minutes 40 seconds in Sanctuary Cove, Australia, on May 11, 2011.

Did You Know?

In an abdominal plank, only the forearms and toes touch the ground. The body is lifted and kept in a straight, plank-like position.

ACTIVITIES

1. The record holder held the position for 33 minutes. Is that more or less than one-half hour? Circle your answer.

   more   **less**

2. A plank is a long, flat board. What could you make with a plank?

   _____

3. Try the abdominal plank position. How long can you hold it? Was it easy or difficult?

   _____

Most Basketball Three-Point Shots in One Minute

Photo: Guinness World Records Limited

Daniel Loriaux (USA) made 25 three-point basketball shots in one minute in Tigard, Oregon, on May 9, 2007.

Did You Know?
NBA player Wilt Chamberlain scored 100 points in a single game for the Philadelphia Warriors in 1962.

ACTIVITIES

1. If a player makes 3 three-point shots and 9 one-point shots during a basketball game, how many points would she score in all?

_____

2. How many points would be scored for 27 three-point shots?

_____

3. How many baskets can you make in one minute?

_____

Most Bounces of a Soap Bubble

Photo: Guinness World Records Limited

At Market Magic Shop in Seattle, Washington, Isaac Louie (USA) bounced a soap bubble 88 times on January 7, 2011.

Did You Know?
Light reflects off the inside and outside of a soap bubble. All these light waves overlap, making rainbow colors appear.

CHECK THIS OUT!

On January 7, 2011, Isaac Louie (United States) bounced into the record books! Louie bounced a tennis ball-sized soap bubble off his hand 88 times before it finally popped, bursting the old record of 38 bounces. Although he only managed to achieve 30 bounces on his first attempt, Louie persevered and tried again to break the record on his second try.

But he's not the only one floating into the record books through bubbles. On April 4, 2011, 118 people in Santa Ana, California, set the world record for the Most People Inside a Soap Bubble. Just a few days later, on April 8, 2011, Sam Sam Bubbleman (United Kingdom) set the record for the Most Soap Bubbles Successfully Blown Inside a Larger Soap Bubble at 56!

1. Louie achieved 30 bounces on his first attempt and 88 bounces on his second attempt. How many bubble bounces did he do in all?

_____

2. If an average adult weighs 160 pounds, what is the likely combined weight of the 118 people inside the soap bubble? Circle the best answer.

   a. 1,880 lb.

   b. 180 lb.

   c. 188,800 lb.

   d. 18,880 lb.

3. Have a bubble gum blowing contest with a friend. Who can blow the biggest bubble?

_____

4. Issac Louie is from Seattle, Washington. The group that set the record for Most People Inside a Soap Bubble is from Santa Ana, California. Find and color the states of Washington and California on this map.

5. Louie persevered when he tried again to set the world record. When was the last time you persevered at something? Write a paragraph about it and explain how it made you feel.

_____

_____

_____

Fastest Time to Duct Tape Yourself to a Wall

Photo: Guinness World Records Limited

Ashrita Furman (USA) duct taped himself to a wall in 5 minutes 9 seconds. He was suspended there for one minute on December 19, 2010.

Did You Know?
Duct tape has been used to patch shoes and make wallets. Astronauts have even used it for emergency repairs.

ACTIVITIES

1. The record took five minutes, nine seconds. How many fewer seconds would make it four-and-a-half minutes?

_____

2. Draw something you could make with these materials: duct tape, shoebox, cotton balls, sandpaper, paint.

Most Basketball Free Throws Made in One Minute

Photo: Guinness World Records Limited

On January 9, 2010, Bob J. Fisher (USA) made 50 free throws in one minute in Blue Rapids, Kansas.

Did You Know?
In setting the record, Fisher attempted 59 free throws and made 50 of them.

ACTIVITIES

1. The word *basketball* is a compound word made up of two smaller words. Write these words on the lines to make more compound words with *ball*: *base*, *foot*, *volley*, *soft*.

   _____ball   _____ball

   _____ball   _____ball

2. How many times can you throw a wad of paper into a basket in one minute? Ask a friend to time you.

   _____

Most Touches of a Soccer Ball With Soles of the Feet in One Minute

Photo: Guinness World Records Limited

At halftime of a 2010 match, Ash Randall (UK) touched a soccer ball 220 times in one minute with the soles of his feet.

Did You Know?

In most of the world, the game of kicking goals is called *football* or *association football*. *Soccer* comes from the abbreviation *assoc*.

ACTIVITIES

1. The record holder touched the ball 220 times. What is $\frac{1}{4}$ of 220?

   _____

2. *Homophones* are words that sound alike but have different meanings and spellings. The words *sole* and *soul* are homophones. Write a homophone below each word.

   <u>   blew   </u>   <u>   flour   </u>

   _____   _____

Most Chicken Nuggets Eaten in Three Minutes

Photo: Guinness World Records Limited

Jordon Ryan (UK) ate 10.16 oz. (287.9 g) of chicken nuggets in three minutes in Manchester, United Kingdom. He ate a total of 17 nuggets.

Did You Know?

Most chickens will stop laying eggs when the weather gets cold. When it warms up, they will start laying again.

ACTIVITIES

1. For each category, write what else you would eat with chicken nuggets for a balanced meal.

   Meat (Protein): _____ chicken nuggets _____

   Dairy: _____

   Vegetable or Fruit: _____

   Vegetable or Fruit: _____

2. The record holder ate 17 nuggets. How many more would he have to eat to reach 25?

   _____

Most Decks of Playing Cards Memorized on Single Sighting

On April 2, 2007, Dave Farrow (Canada) memorized a random sequence of 59 separate packs of cards (3,068 cards) after seeing them just once.

Photo: Guinness World Records Limited

Did You Know?
There are 52 cards in an average deck of playing cards.

CHECK THIS OUT!

Do you have any phone numbers memorized? Science experiments have shown that a normal person can memorize about seven items in a row, which is the length of a standard telephone number. Dave Farrow (Canada), however, has proven that he can memorize much more than that!

During his attempt to set the record for Most Decks of Playing Cards Memorized on Single Sighting, Farrow memorized 3,068 cards in a row after seeing them just once! Farrow only made one error during the entire attempt, which took 4 hours, 58 minutes, 20 seconds. He quickly corrected his mistake before moving on.

1. Look at these five cards for one minute. Say their numbers aloud.

2. Use your hand to cover the cards above. Now, draw them from memory.

3. Try it again! Look at these five cards for one minute. Say their numbers aloud.

4. Use your hand to cover the cards above. Now, draw them from memory.

5. Each deck of 52 cards has 13 cards in each of the four suits—hearts, spades, clubs, and diamonds. If Farrow memorized 3,068 cards, about how many cards were there of each suit?

_____

Most Stairs Climbed in One Minute While Balancing Books on the Head

Photo: Guinness World Records Limited

The most stairs climbed in one minute while balancing books on the head is 122. It was achieved by Ashrita Furman (USA) in 2009.

Did You Know?

Furman ran up three flights of stairs in the New York City subway while balancing about 8 lb. (3.6 kg) of books on his head.

ACTIVITIES

1. Count the steps in a flight of stairs. About how many times would you have to climb it to reach 122 steps?

   _____

2. Balance a book on your head. How many steps can you take before it falls?

   _____

3. How many flights of stairs does your school have?

   _____

Longest Bicycle Stoppie (Feet on Handlebars)

Photo: Guinness World Records Limited

The longest front-wheel bicycle stoppie with feet on handlebars was 57 ft. 4.97 in. It was done by Abdul Rahaman (India) in 2011.

Did You Know?

The distance was measured by marking the points at which the back wheel of the bicycle left the ground and then touched back down.

ACTIVITIES

1. Do a stoppie with a toy vehicle. How many inches did the vehicle travel before its back wheels touched the ground?

2. Design a license plate for your bike or scooter.

Most T-shirts Worn at Once

Photo: Guinness World Records Limited

Krunoslav Budiselić (Croatia) wore 245 T-shirts at once on May 22, 2010. The shirts ranged in size from M to 10XL.

Did You Know?

Could your T-shirt power your smart phone? Energy-transmitting yarn could be made into batteries you can wear.

ACTIVITIES

Design a T-shirt.

Most Custard Pies Thrown in One Minute (Two People)

Photo: Guinness World Records Limited

The most custard pies thrown in one minute is 56. Bipin Larkin (USA) was the thrower and Ashrita Furman (USA) was the catcher in New York City, New York, on April 7, 2010.

Did You Know?

Getting a pie in the face is common in slapstick comedy. Slapstick is a comedy style that includes physical actions and silly situations.

ACTIVITIES

1. In one minute, 56 pies were thrown. How many pies could be thrown in three minutes?

_____

2. Do a comedy routine with a friend. Make a video or perform it live. What is funniest about your show?

_____

3. Would you rather be the pie thrower or the pie catcher? Why?

_____

Most Eggs Cracked With One Hand in One Hour

Photo: Guinness World Records Limited

Bob Blumer (Canada) cracked 2,069 eggs with one hand in one hour on June 24, 2010, in Quebec, Canada.

Did You Know?

A fresh egg will sink in water, and a stale one will float.

CHECK THIS OUT!

Eggs are a good source of protein for a healthy breakfast. There are several ways to prepare eggs—scrambled, fried, and poached, to name a few. Some people enjoy eating eggs in omelets or in egg salad sandwiches.

Bob Blumer (Canada) has found another use for eggs. He has found his way into the record books not by eating them or cooking them, but by cracking them!

Blumer set a world record for cracking 2,069 eggs with one hand in only one hour. He actually cracked 2,318 eggs during the attempt, but 249 were disqualified because their shells fell into the bowl.

ACTIVITIES

1. Conduct an egg-speriment! Ask an adult to give you a hard-boiled egg and a raw egg. Can you tell which one is hard-boiled? How? Make your prediction now.

   _____

2. Test it out! Lay both eggs down on a flat surface and spin them like a top. The raw egg will wobble. The hard-boiled egg will spin. Then, touch each egg lightly as it spins. The raw egg will start moving again after you've tried to stop it, but the hard-boiled egg will stop spinning completely. Was your prediction correct?

   _____

3. You may like scrambled eggs, but do you like scrambled words? Use the clues to unscramble words you read on page 118.

   - layers of eggs cooked with meat, cheese, or vegetables

     tolseem　　　_____

   - an egg's outer covering

     elshl　　　_____

   - meal when eggs are often eaten

     tabfersak　　　_____

   - cooked in boiling water

     cedpoha　　　_____

   - type of food we get from meat and eggs

     notriep　　　_____

   - how Humpty Dumpty was after the fall

     drakecc　　　_____

   - disallowed from competition

     fedsiaqiludi　　　_____

Longest Beach Volleyball Playing Marathon

Photo: Guinness World Records Limited

Four Germans (Mateusz Baca, Sebastian Lüdke, Tomasz Olszak, and Wojciech Kurczyński) played beach volleyball for 25 hours 39 minutes in July 2010.

Did You Know?

Injuries are rare in beach volleyball. The soft sand provides a cushion.

ACTIVITIES

1. Did the teams play for less than or more than one whole day? Circle your answer.

   less than one day   **more than one day**

2. What are your favorite things to do at the beach?

   _____

3. A beach volleyball team has two players. How many players are on 14 beach volleyball teams?

   _____

Largest Gathering of People Dressed as Mobile Phones

At an event in San Juan, Puerto Rico, on November 14, 2007, 275 people dressed as mobile phones.

Photo: Guinness World Records Limited

Did You Know?
A typical South Korean teenager sends over 200,000 text messages each year.

ACTIVITIES

Mobile phones are a convenient way to stay in touch and access information. However, they can also be distracting, especially at school or while driving a car. Do you think children younger than age 14 should have mobile phones of their own? Write three reasons to support your opinion.

_____

_____

_____

_____

130回転超えなるか
世界記録に

Photo: Guinness World Records Limited

Aichi Ono (Japan) spun on his head 135 times in one minute on the set of a TV show on November 18, 2010.

Did You Know?
Doing handstands can build strength and flexibility.

ACTIVITIES

1. How many $20 bills, $10 bills, $5 bills, and $1 bills would you need to make $135?

$20 _____ $5 _____

$10 _____ $1 _____

2. Imagine you are upside down, walking on the ceiling. Write what you see.

_____

_____

Most Sandcastles Built in One Hour

Photo: Guinness World Records Limited

The Lewis-Manning Hospice group (UK) built 539 sandcastles in one hour at Sandbanks Beach in Poole, England, United Kingdom, in 2010.

Did You Know?

Master sandcastle builders use tools such as drinking straws (for blowing sand), paintbrushes, spray bottles, and plastic knives.

ACTIVITIES

1. The group built 539 sandcastles. Is that more or less than $\frac{1}{2}$ of 1,000?

    more than half of 1,000   **less than half of 1,000**

2. Draw what you would build in the sand.

Fastest Time to Arrange a Deck of Playing Cards

Photo: Guinness World Records Limited

Zdeněk Bradáč (Czech Republic) arranged a deck of shuffled playing cards in 36.16 seconds.

Did You Know?

A deck of playing cards has 52 cards divided into four suits: red hearts, black clubs, red diamonds, and black spades.

ACTIVITIES

1. Write the name of a card game you know how to play.

_____

2. With a friend, shuffle a deck of cards. How many minutes does it take you to sort the cards into four suits?

_____

3. How many kings are in a deck of cards?

_____

Photo: Guinness World Records Limited

UNUSUAL ODDITIES

Photo: Guinness World Records Limited

Most One-Hand Jumps (Breakdancing)

Photo: Guinness World Records Limited

Victor Mengarelli (Sweden) completed 93 one-hand jumps during the Guinness World Records Tour 2007 in Haninge, Sweden, on November 2, 2007.

Did You Know?
Each year, 16 of the world's best B-Boys compete at the Red Bull Breakdance Championship One event in a one-on-one competition.

ACTIVITIES

1. Breakdancing is an acrobatic style of dance related to gymnastics and martial arts. Make up a breakdancing routine. Name your dance.

   _____

2. Can you jump 93 times without stopping? Circle your answer.

   yes   **no**

3. Try to do a simple activity, like putting on your shoe, with just one hand. Describe your experience.

   _____

Longest Lawn Mower Ride

Photo: Guinness World Records Limited

Gary Hatter (USA) rode a lawn mower 14,594.5 mi. (23,487.5 km). He started in Portland, Maine, on May 31, 2000, and finished in Daytona Beach, Florida, on February 14, 2001.

Did You Know?

Before the invention of the lawn mower, people with grassy lawns had to use sheep or cattle to "cut" their grass.

ACTIVITIES

1. The lawn mower traveled about 15,000 miles. What is $\frac{1}{3}$ of 15,000?

_____

2. Hatter began his journey in May and ended in February. For about how many months did he ride?

_____

3. If you earn $15 for each yard you mow, how much will you earn for mowing 11 yards?

_____

Largest Teddy Bear Sculpture

Photo: Guinness World Records Limited

Yankee Doodle Teddy made its first appearance at a 1989 Disney World Teddy Bear Convention. Seated, it is 24 ft. (7.3 m) tall; standing, it is 32 ft. (9.75 m) tall.

Did You Know?
The teddy bear got its name from President Theodore "Teddy" Roosevelt in 1902.

ACTIVITIES

1. How much taller is Yankee Doodle Teddy when it is standing (32 feet) than when it is sitting (24 feet)?

_____

2. Did you ever have a favorite stuffed animal or toy? Circle words that describe it.

old	**giant**	**friendly**
soft	**new**	**torn**
fluffy	**cute**	**small**

Longest Ladder

Photo: Guinness World Records Limited

In April 2005, a 120-rung, 135 ft. (41.16 m) long ladder was completed by the Handwerks Museum, St. Leonhard, Austria.

Did You Know?
Some believe that the space formed between a ladder and the wall it leans against contains evil spirits, which is why some people think it is bad luck to walk under a ladder.

ACTIVITIES

1. How long is your stride? Step out with one foot, then freeze. Ask a friend to measure the distance between your two feet.

   _____

2. The record-breaking ladder is 135 feet long. How many strides would you need to take to equal about 135 feet?

   _____

3. Write where you would climb if you had a giant ladder.

   _____

Largest Game of Pick-Up Sticks

Photo: Guinness World Records Limited

Students in Harare, Zimbabwe, played a game of pick-up sticks with sticks that measured 29 ft. 10 in. (9.1 m) long and 5.7 in. (14.5 cm) in diameter on July 21, 2007.

Did You Know?
The first form of pick-up sticks was used in China to make predictions.

CHECK THIS OUT!

A group of high school students in Zimbabwe set a world record by playing the Largest Game of Pick-Up Sticks ever. The sticks were about as long as a telephone pole and almost as wide as a gallon of paint!

Pick-up sticks is an old game. People around the world have played it for hundreds of years. The rules and scoring vary from place to place, but the idea is the same. In the United States, the game usually has 25 to 30 sticks with four or five different colors. To start the game, you hold the sticks upright, then let them drop. The sticks fall at random. The goal is to remove a stick from the pile without moving any other sticks. The first player to reach a certain number of points wins.

1. What does *random* mean? Circle the best definition.

   a. without a plan, pattern, or purpose

   b. carefully arranged

   c. out of control

   d. messy

2. In what two ways would it be challenging to play pick-up sticks with giant sticks?

   _____

   _____

3. With a friend, use drinking straws and tape to make a few giant "sticks" about three feet long. Make up a game to play with the sticks. What is the name of your game?

   _____

4. Children have played pick-up sticks for hundreds of years. Interview your parents and grandparents. Circle games they used to play when they were kids. Put a star by circled games that you like to play.

hide-and-seek	**tag**	**video games**
marbles	**jump rope**	**jacks**
pick-up sticks	**hopscotch**	**four square**

5. Look at a map of Africa. What four countries border the country of Zimbabwe?

   _____   _____

   _____   _____

Largest Motorized Shopping Cart

Photo: Guinness World Records Limited

Edd China (UK) displayed a motorized shopping cart that measured 9 ft. 10 in. (3 m) long, 11 ft. 5 in. (3.5 m) tall, and 5 ft. 11 in. (1.8 m) wide, in Watford, United Kingdom, on November 9, 2005.

Did You Know?
Between 500 billion and 1 trillion plastic shopping bags are used each year.

ACTIVITIES

1. Write a shopping list of giant items to fill a giant shopping cart.

_____   _____

_____   _____

2. Do you think shopping carts at the grocery store should be motorized? Explain why or why not.

_____

_____

Highest Altitude for a Balloon Skywalk

Photo: Guinness World Records Limited

Mike Howard (UK) walked on a beam between two balloons at an altitude of 21,398 ft. (6,522 m) near Yeovil, Somerset, United Kingdom, on September 1, 2004.

Did You Know?

A sheep, a rooster, and a duck were used to test the first hot air balloon flight.

ACTIVITIES

1. Make a line on the ground with string or sidewalk chalk. Practice balancing on it. How many steps can you take without "falling"?

   _____

2. Build two tall stacks of blocks with a walkway in between. Draw your structure.

Largest Inflatable Beach Ball

Photo: Guinness World Records Limited

The largest inflatable beach ball was 48 ft. 2 in. (14.70 m) in diameter. It was presented in Lagos, Nigeria, on August 10, 2010.

Did You Know?
The ball was measured four separate times. The official diameter is an average of the four measurements.

ACTIVITIES

1. Choose something large to measure, such as a blanket or your bicycle. Measure it three times. Write each measurement below.

   _____   _____   _____

2. What is the average of your three measurements?

   _____

3. If your three measurements were different, what are some reasons that could explain the differences?

   _____

Most Socks Worn on One Foot

Photo: Guinness World Records Limited

Luke G. Cimino (USA) pulled 102 socks onto one foot in Downingtown, Pennsylvania, on January 16, 2009.

Did You Know?

There are socks that are knitted to fit a foot just like a glove fits a hand. They come in different lengths, colors, and designs. Toe socks are commonly worn with sandals and flip-flops.

ACTIVITIES

1. Ask your parent for 10 socks. Have a contest with a friend. Who can put five socks on one foot in the shortest time?

_____

2. Who says socks have to match? Decorate these socks with colors and patterns.

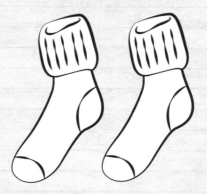

Largest Underpants

Photo: Guinness World Records Limited

Angajala Venkata Giri (India) presented a pair of underpants that measured 58 ft. 3 in. (17.75 m) wide and 38 ft. 10 in. (11.82 m) tall in Jeypore, India, on December 15, 2007.

Did You Know?

During World War II, there was a rubber and metal shortage, so undergarments had buttons and fasteners instead of elastic.

CHECK THIS OUT!

Underpants are supposed to be worn under clothes. Angajala Venkata Giri, a tailor who lives in India, had another idea. He sewed the Largest Underpants in the world. It took the 60-year-old man five days before he finished the underpants on December 15, 2007. When held up, they measured 58 feet, 3 inches across the waist. Giri used 492 yards of cloth to make these big bottoms!

It also took only five days to create the world's Longest Necktie. Members of the Academia Cravatica organization created a necktie measuring 2,650 feet. Upon completion, it was tied around an arena in Pula, Croatia, on October 18, 2003.

1. If Giri finished the underpants on December 15, 2007, on what date did he begin sewing?

   _____

2. If Giri bought the fabric for $4.00 per yard, how much did he spend?

   a. $19,680.00

   b. $9.68

   c. $1,968.00

   d. $19.68

3. If the underpants are held open, what is the circumference of the waist of the world's Largest Underpants?

   _____

4. Estimate how many times the world's Longest Necktie would wrap around the circumference of the world's Largest Underpants' waistband.

   _____

5. The word *underpants* is a compound word made from two smaller words. Use these smaller words to write four more compound words: *sweat, coat, ear, swim, shirt, rain, muffs, suit.*

   _____   _____

   _____   _____

6. How many times can you say this tongue twister fast?

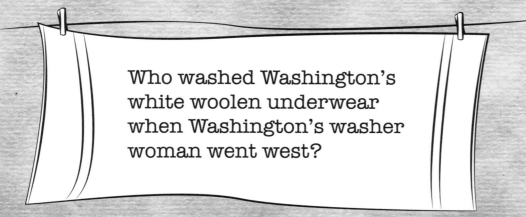

Who washed Washington's white woolen underwear when Washington's washer woman went west?

Largest Dog Back Stall

Photo: Guinness World Records Limited

Twelve dogs jumped up and stood on the backs of their handlers simultaneously at the Oregon State Barks Day event in Corbett, Oregon, on July 31, 2004.

Did You Know?

The United States Dog Agility Association (USDAA) has more than 25,000 dogs as registered competitors.

ACTIVITIES

1. The word *simultaneous* means "at the same time." For how many seconds can you pat your head and rub your tummy simultaneously?

   _____

2. Think of a simple trick like clapping your hands under one leg. Then, gather as many people as you can. Can everyone do the trick simultaneously? Write what you did.

   _____

   _____

Largest Canned Food Structure

Photo: Guinness World Records Limited

The largest canned food structure consisted of 115,527 cans and was built at the Walt Disney World Resort in Lake Buena Vista, Florida, on February 11, 2010.

Did You Know?

It took volunteers four days to create the structure. The food was donated to food banks and was enough for more than 70,000 meals.

ACTIVITIES

1. If you donate two cans of food each week to a food bank, how many cans will you donate in one year?

   _____

2. Make a structure by stacking non-breakable items such as pillows or paper cups. Write what you did.

   _____

   _____

Largest Pair of Socks

Photo: Guinness World Records Limited

Michael Roy Layne (USA) made a pair of nylon socks that measured 45 ft. (13.72 m) long from top to toe and 10 ft. (3.05 m) wide in October 1986. They were displayed outside of the city hall building in Boston, Massachusetts.

Did You Know?
The Bureau of Missing Socks was formed during the Civil War to hold Union soldiers accountable for the number of socks they used and lost.

ACTIVITIES

1. How many total socks do 19 people wear?

_____

2. Make a pile of 10 socks for you and another pile of 10 for a friend. Have a sock-matching race. Who made five pairs of socks first?

_____

3. Use an old sock to make a puppet. Write what you did.

_____

Largest Button-Down Shirt

Photo: Guinness World Records Limited

The largest button-down shirt was 214 ft. 6 in. (65.39 m) long, with a chest of 172 ft. 11 in. (52.72 m) wide, and sleeves measuring 78 ft. 8 in. by 51 ft. 3 in. (23.98 m by 15.64 m). It was made by Walbusch (Germany), and was measured in Düsseldorf, Germany, on June 25, 2009.

Did You Know?
Rumor has it that King Francis I of France had about 13,600 buttons sewn onto his entire wardrobe.

ACTIVITIES

1. The word *button* begins with *b*. Write more words you know that begin with *b* and have two or more syllables.

   _____   _____   _____

   _____   _____   _____

2. Borrow two large button-down shirts from an adult. Then, have a buttoning contest with a friend. Who buttoned up the shirt fastest?

   _____

Longest Pencil

Photo: Guinness World Records Limited

Ashrita Furman (USA) and members of the Sri Chinmoy Centre in New York City, New York, created a pencil that measured 76 ft. 3 in. (23.23 m) on August 27, 2007.

Did You Know?

Students from local schools in Kuwait made a pencil mosaic that contained 1,025,000 pencils.

CHECK THIS OUT!

Don't worry. You won't have to take a test with this pencil. That's a good thing, because you could never lift it. No one could. The world's Longest Pencil is about as long as a tennis court!

The idea for the pencil came from Ashrita Furman (United States). He gathered a team of 40 volunteers from 20 different countries. The team worked over 12 hours a day for two weeks. Furman did not want something that just looked like a pencil. He wanted a real pencil. He made sure the "lead" in the center was real graphite. This lead was 10 inches thick. It weighed 4,500 pounds. That is as much as a great white shark!

ACTIVITIES

1. The world's Longest Pencil is too heavy to lift. How many pounds do you think it could weigh and still be usable?

   _____

2. We often say that pencils contain lead, but the core of a pencil is actually made of graphite. *Graphite* is a crystalline material found in Earth's crust. It is a form of an element that is one of the most abundant materials in the entire universe, and which forms the basis for all life. Circle the name of this element.

   carbon   **boron**

   sulfur   **calcium**

3. If you were going to build a giant object to set a world record, what would you build?

   _____

4. The Statue of Liberty's right arm, which holds the torch, is 42 feet long. How many more inches long is the longest pencil?

   _____

5. What kind of doodles could you draw with a giant pencil? Use your pencil to finish this doodle.

Longest Canoe

Photo: Guinness World Records Limited

Students and teachers in Newport, Maine, built a canoe that is 149 ft. 1 in. (45.44 m) long. It was presented on July 8, 2006.

Did You Know?
Archaeologists discovered an 8,000-year-old dugout canoe in ancient ruins in China.

ACTIVITIES

1. Use aluminum foil to make a canoe that floats in the sink or bathtub. How many inches long is your canoe?

   _____

2. How many times can you say this tongue twister quickly: *Can you canoe a canoe?*

   _____

3. Ancient people used canoes to explore the oceans. Use a world map or globe to find an island you would like to visit. Write the island's name.

   _____

Largest Rubber Band Ball

Photo: Guinness World Records Limited

Joel Waul (USA) presented a rubber band ball that measured 6 ft. 7 in. (200.7 cm) high and weighed 9,032 lb. (4,097 kg) in Lauderhill, Florida, on November 13, 2008. He began making the ball in 2004.

Did You Know?

Waul sold his rubber band ball to Ripley's Believe It or Not museums in 2009. It took a crane, a flatbed truck, and a transportation team to move the ball.

ACTIVITIES

1. With a friend, collect some favorite or unusual items to place in a mini-museum. Create a label for each item and invite guests to visit. Write a name for your museum.

   _____

2. A 3-D circle shape, like a rubber band ball, is called a *sphere*. Look all around for spheres. List what you find.

   _____   _____

   _____   _____

Most Air Guitar World Championship Wins

Zac "The Magnet" Monro (UK) and Ochi "Dainoji" Yosuke (Japan) have each won two Air Guitar World Championships at the Oulu Music Video Festival.

Photo: Guinness World Records Limited

Did You Know?
Oddly enough, the winner of the Air Guitar World Championship receives a real guitar.

ACTIVITIES

1. With adult help, cut a hole in an empty cereal box. Stretch a few rubber bands across the hole to make a guitar. Write what you can do with your guitar.

   _____

2. When you and a friend watch TV, play air guitar to the music during commercials. Do you think this is a good way to get exercise? Explain why or why not.

   _____

Largest Rocking Chair

Photo: Guinness World Records Limited

Dan Sanzaro presented a rocking chair measuring 42 ft. 1 in. (12.83 m) tall and 20 ft. 3 in. (6.17 m) wide in Cuba, Missouri, on September 4, 2008.

Did You Know?

President John F. Kennedy used rocking chairs to help relieve his back pain. He even had a rocking chair on Air Force One.

ACTIVITIES

1. The largest rocking chair is 20 feet wide. Circle enough 5s to add up to 20. Draw an X through 5s that are not needed.

   5   **5**   **5**   **5**   **5**

2. Imagine you are a giant. Write what you would think about while rocking in your giant rocking chair.

   _____

   _____

Most Stamps Licked in One Minute

Nepal

Deepak Sharma Bajagain (Nepal) licked 70 stamps in one minute in Balkumari, Lalitpur, Nepal, on August 6, 2010.

Photo: Guinness World Records Limited

Did You Know?
Stamp collecting as a hobby is called *philately*.

CHECK THIS OUT!

Stamp collecting is a popular hobby for both children and adults Collectors sometimes keep their stamps in albums because that keeps them from getting damaged. Some stamp collectors like stamps that are very old, or those that are from faraway places. Their stamps may be brand new or they may have traveled through the mail. Sometimes, stamps can be worth a lot of money, especially those that were printed incorrectly.

Deepak Sharma Bajagain (Nepal) probably collected stamps, but for a different reason. In August 2010, he licked 70 stamps in one minute and placed them on envelopes. He actually licked 71 stamps in the allotted time, but one envelope was disqualified because the stamp fell off before counting began.

ACTIVITIES

1. *Antonyms* are words with opposite meanings. Read each word below. Then, find its antonym in the word bank and write it in the boxes. To find the answer to the riddle, read the letters in the bold boxes.

expensive

part

noisy

clean

toss

safe

end

shrink

child

scared

forget

serious

Word Bank:
adult
whole
brave
begin
remember
dangerous
silent
stretch
cheap
playful
filthy
catch

Riddle: What travels all around the world, yet always stays in the corner?

A ___ ___ ___ ___ ___ ___ ___ ___ ___ ___ ___ ___

2. What do you like to collect? Explain why.

_____

_____

3. Why do you think stamps that were printed incorrectly are worth a lot of money? Explain your answer.

_____

_____

Longest Time Spinning a *Guinness World Records*® Book on Finger

Aaron Sass (USA) spun a *Guinness World Records* book on one finger for 6 minutes 50.11 seconds in Lodi, California, on January 16, 2010.

Photo: Guinness World Records Limited

Did You Know?
The *Guinness World Records* book was introduced on August 27, 1955. It became Britain's number one bestseller by Christmas that year.

ACTIVITIES

1. Practice spinning three things on one finger: a ball, a playing card, and this book. Which is easiest to spin?

_____

2. After practicing, write your best tip that would help other people learn to spin things on their fingers.

_____

3. How many times can you spin this book on your finger?

_____

Largest Padlock

Photo: Guinness World Records Limited

Students and teachers in Nizhny Novgorod, Russia, created a lock that measures 56.8 in. (144.3 cm) tall, 41.3 in. (105 cm) wide, and 10.2 in. (26 cm) deep. Including the key, the giant security lock weighs 916 lb. (415.5 kg).

Did You Know?
Brent Dixon (USA) has a keychain collection of 41,418 different key chains. He has been collecting them since 2001.

ACTIVITIES

1. Write words you know that rhyme with *key*.

_____   _____   _____

_____   _____   _____

2. Draw a fun keychain for this key.

Furthest Distance Jumping on a Pogo Stick

Photo: Guinness World Records Limited

Ashrita Furman (USA) covered a distance of 23.11 mi. (37.18 km) on a pogo stick in Bayside, New York, on June 22, 1997. It took him 12 hours 27 minutes to complete the task.

Did You Know?
In 1920, a marriage ceremony was performed on pogo sticks.

ACTIVITIES

1. Furman jumped 23 miles on a pogo stick. Find out what place is about 23 miles from your home. Use a map or ask an adult. Write the name of the place.

   _____

2. Furman's journey took 12 hours. Find out what place is about 12 hours away from you. Would you take a car, boat, or plane to get there?

   _____

Largest Word Search Puzzle

Photo: Guinness World Records Limited

Rackspace Hosting, Inc. (Texas) created a word search puzzle measuring 21 ft. 3 in. (6.47 m) by 18 ft. (5.49 m) on July 6, 2009.

Did You Know?

The largest word search puzzle had a total of 25,112 letters.

ACTIVITIES

Find a big writing surface like a sheet of newspaper, a marker board, or your driveway (if you use sidewalk chalk). Cover the surface with a giant puzzle for your friend to do. Write about your puzzle and draw part of it below.

_____

_____

Largest Ball of Plastic Wrap

Photo: Guinness World Records Limited

Jake Lonsway (USA) created a ball of plastic wrap that measured 11 ft. 6 in. (3.51 m) in circumference and weighed 281 lb. 8 oz. (127.7 kg).

Did You Know?

Richard Roman (USA) made a giant ball of aluminum foil that weighed 1,615 lb. (732.5 kg).

CHECK THIS OUT!

Jake Lonsway (United States) is one of the youngest Guinness World Records record-holders. He was just seven years old when he set the record for the Largest Ball of Plastic Wrap. It took Lonsway eight months to create the ball that measured 138 inches in circumference, and is about the size of a large exercise ball.

Lonsway and his parents had wanted to find a record that Lonsway could try to beat. They found the record for a ball of plastic wrap, which, at the time, was 250 pounds. Soon after that, Lonsway's mother brought home a ball of plastic wrap the size of a softball. Lonsway kept adding more plastic wrap to the ball as it grew and grew. After setting the record, the ball was moved to a children's museum in Michigan, where it remains today.

ACTIVITIES

Complete the crossword puzzle with words you read on page 154.

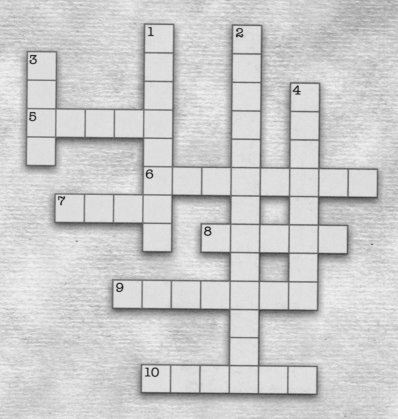

Across

5. Number of months it took Lonsway to create the ball

6. Material used for Richard Roman's ball

7. Lonsway created a ____ of plastic wrap.

8. Lonsway's age when he set the record

9. Lonsway holds the record for the ____ ball of plastic wrap.

10. Where you can see the Largest Ball of Plastic Wrap on display today

Down

1. Size of the plastic wrap ball that Lonsway's mother brought home

2. The distance around the outside of a sphere

3. The ball grew and ____.

4. Lonsway is one of the ____ Guinness World Records® record-holders.

Heaviest Mantle of Bees

Photo: Guinness World Records Limited

Vipin Seth (India) wore a mantle of about 613,500 bees weighing 135 lb. 5 oz. (61.4 kg) in New Delhi, India, on March 9, 2009.

Did You Know?
It takes 12 bees, collecting nectar from 2,000 flowers, to make a tablespoon of honey!

ACTIVITIES

1. One bee has six legs. How many legs do 17 bees have?

   _____

2. A bee's wings beat 200 times each second, making the special sound that bees make. Write the sound bees make.

   _____

3. There are three types of bees. Workers gather food. Queens lay eggs and tell workers what to do. Drones stay home in the hive. Which kind of bee would you be? Why?

   _____

Largest Pocket Knife

Photo: Guinness World Records Limited

The largest pocket knife measures 12 ft. 9 in. (3.9 m) when open and weighs a total of 269 lb. (122 kg). It was handmade by Virgílio, Raul, and Manuel Pires (all Portugal).

Did You Know?
Over 34,000 Swiss Army knives are manufactured each day.

ACTIVITIES

1. Ask an adult to teach you how to use a knife safely. With adult help, use a pocket knife or paring knife to carve something from a bar of soap. Write what you made.

   _____

2. Some adults keep pocket knives in their pockets. Write a list of things you keep in your pockets.

   _____ _____ _____

   _____ _____ _____

Fastest Towed Toilet

Photo: Guinness World Records Limited

Garrett Olson (USA) towed a toilet at a speed of 49.6 mph (79.83 km/h) in Lancaster, New York, on September 2, 2009.

Did You Know?
The average person uses the restroom 2,500 times each year, for a total of three years over a lifetime.

ACTIVITIES

1. The record-breaking toilet traveled about 50 miles per hour. Circle enough 10s to add up to 50. Draw an X through 10s that are not needed.

    10   **10**   **10**   **10**   **10**   **10**

2. The word *tow* means "to pull." Write a list of things that are commonly towed.

    _____   _____

    _____   _____

Longest Bubble Chain

Photo: Guinness World Records Limited

Sam Sam (UK) created a bubble chain that was 26 bubbles long at the offices of Guinness World Records, London, United Kingdom, on April 12, 2010.

Did You Know?

Just like a bubble, a paper clip will float on the surface of a glass of water. It helps if the paper clip is a little greasy. Try it out!

ACTIVITIES

1. Try a bubble experiment. With an adult's help, fill a glass with water until it is three-quarters full. Pour in one-half inch of vegetable oil. Now, sprinkle in some salt. What happens?

_____

_____

2. Have a bubble-blowing contest with a friend. Who blew the largest bubble?

_____

Largest Pair of Scissors

Photo: Guinness World Records Limited

Neerja Roy Chowdhury (India) unveiled a pair of scissors that measured 7 ft. 7 in. (2.31 m) from tip to handle in New Delhi, India, on August 16, 2009.

Did You Know?

Powerful scissors known as the "Jaws of Life" can cut through a car to help rescue trapped passengers.

CHECK THIS OUT!

Imagine you are a giant. What are some things you might need for school? Well, for starters, you would probably need some of the world's largest school supplies, such as the Largest Scissors and the Largest Ballpoint Pen.

Neerja Roy Chowdhury (India) set a record for her scissors that are 7 feet, 7 inches long. These scissors even work, too! They were used during a ribbon-cutting ceremony in honor of Chowdhury's book being ready to sell.

If you can believe it, the Largest Ballpoint Pen is even bigger! It measures 18 feet, 0.53 inches long and weighs 82.08 pounds, 1.24 ounces. The pen was made by Acharya Makunuri Srinivasa (India) on April 24, 2011.

1. Is the length of the world's Largest Scissors closer to seven feet or eight feet? Circle your answer.

7 feet   **8 feet**

2. What is the length in inches of the world's Largest Scissors?

   a. 910 inches

   b. 91 inches

   c. 9.10 inches

   d. 0.910 inches

3. With the help of an adult, measure a pair of scissors. About how many pairs of your scissors placed end to end would be needed to equal the length of the world's Largest Scissors?

   _____

4. Circle what you would cut with a giant pair of scissors.

   a ribbon for the grand opening of a giant ice cream shop

   a package of giant seeds

   a giant horse's mane

   material to make a giant ladder into space

5. Write a story about your answer to #4.

   _____

   _____

   _____

   _____

   _____

   _____

Largest Thimble

The Pérez brothers (Spain) handmade a copper thimble that is 4.9 in. (12.5 cm) tall and weighs 11.23 oz. (318.46 g) in 2000.

Did You Know?
During World War I, the British government collected silver thimbles and melted them down to buy hospital equipment.

Photo: Guinness World Records Limited

ACTIVITIES

1. How many ounces are in a pound? Does the world's largest thimble weigh more or less than a pound? Circle your answer.

   more than a pound   **less than a pound**

2. A thimble keeps your finger from getting hurt when you sew. Imagine something that will keep you from getting hurt when you play your favorite sport. Draw your invention.

Fastest Time to Escape From Three Handcuffs Under Water

Photo: Guinness World Records Limited

Zdeněk Bradáč (Czech Republic) successfully escaped from three sets of handcuffs while under water in 38.69 seconds in Jablonec nad Nisou, Czech Republic, on September 9, 2009.

Did You Know?

Harry Houdini, an escape artist from the late 19th century, was known as the "Handcuff King."

ACTIVITIES

1. Have a contest with a friend. Dress up in three jackets. Put three pairs of socks on your feet and three more on your hands. Which one of you can "escape" from the extra clothing in 38 seconds?

   _____

2. Bradáč escaped in about 40 seconds. What fraction of a minute is 40 seconds?

   _____

Most Alarm Clocks Smashed With the Feet in One Minute

Photo: Guinness World Records Limited

Jay Wheddon (UK) smashed 88 alarm clocks with his feet during a television show taping in London, United Kingdom, on October 3, 2008.

Did You Know?
The "Flying Alarm Clock" can awaken anyone. To turn it off, you must catch a small propeller that launches from the clock and flies around.

ACTIVITIES

1. With a friend, build 25 or more small block towers to cover the floor. Can you knock them all down with your feet in one minute? Circle your answer.

   yes   **no**

2. Draw hands on the clock face to show what time you wake up for school in the morning.

Largest Broom (T-Shaped)

Photo: Guinness World Records Limited

The largest T-shaped broom measured 38 ft. 3.8 in. (11.68 m) long and 19 ft. 9.8 in. (6.04 m) wide on April 29, 2007, in Bad Schussenried-Kürnbach, Germany.

Did You Know?

There are many superstitions about brooms. Some refer to sweeping evil, unwelcome guests, or even family members out of the house.

ACTIVITIES

1. Write what you do to help clean up around the house.

   _____

2. The largest T-shaped broom is about 38 feet long. An average broom is about three feet long. How much longer than an average broom is the largest broom?

   _____

3. Help someone you know by sweeping a porch or walkway without being asked. Write what you did.

   _____

Largest Bar of Soap

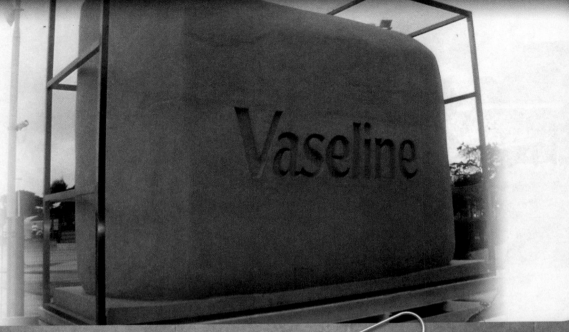

Photo: Guinness World Records Limited

A bar of soap weighing 27,557 lb. (12,500 kg) was presented in Durban, South Africa, on August 12, 2005.

Did You Know?

Ivory bar soap is known as the "soap that floats." All other bar soaps sink.

CHECK THIS OUT!

Rub-a-dub, you are ready to scrub! Now, where is that bar of soap? If you are reaching for the world's Largest Bar of Soap, you will need help to lift it, and it probably won't fit in your bathtub, either. This bar of soap, made by a company in South Africa, weighs 27,557 pounds! It measures 13.4 feet long and 8.2 feet wide. Its height is 4.5 feet.

Someone who is large enough to use the Largest Bar of Soap may also need the world's Largest Beach Towel to dry off! The beach towel measured 285 feet, 10 inches long and 82 feet, 8 inches wide and was displayed in Las Palmas, Gran Canaria, Spain, on June 5, 2010. This towel is even bigger than the former Largest Beach Towel, which was 210 feet, 8 inches long and 101 feet, 9 inches wide.

1. What does *former* mean? Circle the best definition.

   a. previous

   b. current

   c. best

   d. unimportant

2. Write a sentence that includes the word *former*.

   _____

3. There are 2,000 pounds in a ton. How many tons does the world's Largest Bar of Soap weigh? Write an equation to show how you know.

   _____

4. Round the measurements of the world's Largest Bar of Soap to the nearest whole numbers. What is the area of the largest face of the soap? Use this diagram to help you.

   _____ **feet**

   _____ **feet**   **area = _____**   _____ **feet**

   _____ **feet**

5. Round the measurements of the world's Largest Beach Towel to the nearest whole numbers. What is its perimeter? Use this diagram to help you.

   _____ **feet**

   _____ **feet**   **perimeter = _____**   _____ **feet**

   _____ **feet**

Most Crash Tests

Photo: Guinness World Records Limited

W.R. "Rusty" Haight (USA) had endured 718 collisions in cars as a "human crash test dummy" by February 2003.

Did You Know?

There is a new computer model of a crash test dummy that has detailed reproductions of the human body—including internal organs, ligaments, blood vessels, skin, and bones.

ACTIVITIES

1. Decorate a toilet paper tube to make a toy car. Use paper fasteners to attach wheels. Make up a crash test for your car. Explain what happened.

_____

2. A *collision* is "a clash between two things." Unfortunately, cars have collisions. Football players collide, too. Name other things that sometimes crash.

_____   _____

Largest Sandal

Photo: Guinness World Records Limited

A sandal measuring 21 ft. 8 in. (6.6 m) long, 6 ft. 6 in. (2 m) wide, and 11 ft. 6 in. (3.5 m) high was created on September 4, 2008, by Nelson Jimenez Flores (Columbia).

Did You Know?

Louise Hollis's (USA) toenails were a combined length of 7 ft. 3 in. (2.21 m) in 1991. She has to wear open-toed shoes so they don't drag on the ground.

ACTIVITIES

1. The Largest Sandal is about 21 feet long. How many groups of 7 are in 21?

_____

2. Most ceilings are eight feet tall. How much taller is the sandal than an eight-foot ceiling?

_____

3. Who in your family wears the largest shoes?

_____

Longest Time Restraining a Car

Photo: Guinness World Records Limited

Franz Muellner (Austria) restrained a vehicle on full power for 13.84 seconds in Mexico City, Mexico, on July 28, 2008.

Did You Know?

Strong man Muellner holds other Guinness World Records. On November 19, 2009, he rolled a car nine times in four minutes five seconds.

ACTIVITIES

1. Set a kitchen timer for 14 seconds. Challenge yourself to do something in that time, such as zipping up and putting on your backpack. What challenge did you complete?

_____

2. Muellner stopped a car. Write a story about a superhero who stops something bad from happening.

_____

_____

Largest Wooden Chest

Photo: Guinness World Records Limited

In June 2005, Glen Jorgensen (Norway) made a wooden chest that is 13 ft. 1 in. (4 m) long, 6 ft. 7 in. (2 m) tall, and 7 ft. 10 in. (2.4 m) deep in Fevik, Norway.

Did You Know?

So it wouldn't be noticed, pirate loot was not stored in treasure chests but in plain wooden crates that were nailed shut.

ACTIVITIES

1. Imagine what giant toys you would keep in a giant toy chest. List them.

   _____   _____

   _____   _____

2. Read above to see how long, tall, and deep the Largest Wooden Chest is. Would the Largest Teddy Bear Sculpture (page 128) fit inside the box? Circle your answer.

   yes   **no**

Largest Jigsaw Puzzle

Photo: Guinness World Records Limited

A jigsaw puzzle measuring 58,435 sq. ft. (5,428.8 m²) was constructed in Hong Kong on November 3, 2002. The puzzle consisted of 21,600 pieces and took 777 people to assemble.

Did You Know?

In the 1760s, the first jigsaw puzzles were made from maps to teach geography.

CHECK THIS OUT!

Many people like doing jigsaw puzzles. No jigsaw puzzle, however, is bigger than the one put together in Hong Kong. This puzzle was about the size of a football field!

The very first jigsaw puzzle may have been made by John Spilsbury in the 1700s. Spilsbury took a map of Europe and cut it up to form puzzle pieces. One hundred years later, people began to cut puzzle pieces with a special saw. These were the first true jigsaw puzzles.

People today still like jigsaw puzzles. Doing a puzzle can help relieve stress. It is a nice way to spend time with friends and it helps keep your mind sharp. Even if your next puzzle does not have 21,600 pieces, it can still be a fun challenge!

ACTIVITIES

1. John Spilsbury made the first puzzle by cutting up a _____.

2. Would you rather do a jigsaw puzzle by yourself or be one of the 777 people to put together the world's Largest Jigsaw Puzzle? Explain your answer.

_____

_____

_____

3. Circle your favorite types of puzzles.

      crossword puzzle   **word search**

      Sudoku   **hangman**

      mazes   **word scrambles**

4. Find two puzzles with about the same number of pieces. Have a puzzle contest with a friend. Who worked the puzzle fastest?

_____

5. Now, choose one puzzle to work together with your friend. Time yourselves. Which was faster— the best individual time or the combined time? Write the name(s) of the winner or winners on the ribbon.

Largest Clapboard

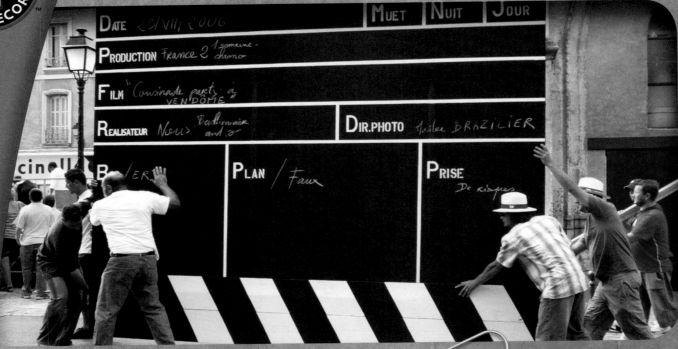

Photo: Guinness World Records Limited

The world's largest clapboard measured 10 ft. 2 in. (3.11 m) tall and 13 ft. 2 in. (4 m) wide. It was created in Vendome, France, on July 29, 2006.

Did You Know?

The first movie theater opened on June 19, 1905, in Pittsburgh, Pennsylvania. It was named the *Nickelodeon*.

ACTIVITIES

1. Imagine you woke up one day to find you had grown 10 feet tall. Write a movie script about it. Write the name of your movie.

_____

2. Choose one adjective and one noun to write the name of a movie you would like to watch.

Adjectives	Stupendous	Hair-raising	Menacing
Nouns	Theater	Mountain	Whales

_____

Largest Whoopee Cushion

Photo: Guinness World Records Limited

Steve Mesure (UK) created a whoopee cushion that measured 10 ft. (3.05 m) in diameter in London, United Kingdom, on June 14, 2008.

Did You Know?

The whoopee cushion has also been called a *Poo-Poo Cushion, Whoopee Pillow,* and *Boop-Boopa Doop.*

ACTIVITIES

1. The *diameter* of a circle tells the length of a line drawn through its center. Draw a circle with a one-inch diameter.

2. Whoopee cushions are used to play jokes on friends. Play a fun, safe joke on a friend, such as setting an alarm clock to go off in the middle of the night. Write what you did.

Photo: Guinness World Records Limited

Oliver Gratzer (Austria) threw 27 domestic appliances in one minute during a television show in Rome, Italy, on March 18, 2010.

Did You Know?

Rick Smith Jr. (USA) threw a single playing card 216 ft. 4 in. (65.96 m) on March 21, 2002.

ACTIVITIES

1. Gather cotton balls, stuffed animals, or other soft objects. How many can you throw in one minute?

_____

2. Gratzer threw 27 appliances. How many groups of 3 are in 27?

_____

3. What home appliance do you use most often?

_____

Longest Distance Covered by a Car Driven on Two Side Wheels

Photo: Guinness World Records Limited

Michele Pilia (Italy) drove a car on its side on two wheels for a total distance of 230.57 mi. (371.06 km) in Cagliari, Italy, on February 26, 2009.

Did You Know?

Approximately 5 to 7 million tires caught fire on October 31, 1983, in Rhinehart, Virginia. The fire was put out, but the tires smoldered for six months.

ACTIVITIES

1. Pilia drove the car for 230 miles. What is $\frac{1}{5}$ of 230?

   _____

2. Things that are stable are unlikely to fall. Explain why a tricycle is more stable than a bicycle.

   _____

   _____

3. Play with a toy car. For how many seconds can you make it go on its two side wheels?

   _____

Fastest Furniture

Photo: Guinness World Records Limited

Marek Turowski (UK) achieved a speed of 92 mph (148 km/h) while driving a motorized sofa in Leicestershire, United Kingdom, on May 11, 2007.

Did You Know?

The largest inflatable couch was 67 ft. 3 in. (20.5 m) long, 26 ft. 7 in. (8.1 m) wide, and 26 ft. 7 in. (8.1 m) tall.

CHECK THIS OUT!

This couch has no place in a living room. It was made for the road! Edd China created the speedy sofa that holds the Guinness World Record for Fastest Furniture. It went 92 miles per hour!

Marek Turowski (United Kingdom) is a 38-year-old gardener who lives in London. He won an online auction for the chance to drive the sofa. The money raised from the auction went to a foundation for medical research.

In addition to the sofa, China has built many extraordinary vehicles. He has made a moving garden shed, a moving bathroom, and an alien spacecraft. China has broken other records, including the world's Fastest Office. The office included a desk, four chairs, a computer, and a water cooler. It reached a speed of 87 miles per hour.

Complete the statements by writing words you read on page 178. Then look in the puzzle to find the words you wrote. Search across and down.

The motorized sofa achieved a _____ of 92 mph.

Another word for *sofa* is _____.

The record-setting sofa is _____ so it will drive on the road.

The record is for the world's _____ _____.

Turowski lives in the city of _____.

An _____ was held to decide who would drive the sofa.

China built moving versions of a shed, a spacecraft, and a _____.

The fastest furniture is not built for the living room, but for the _____.

China's creations are not ordinary. They are _____.

```
d o a r r b u o o a e e s
h e f a r a a a m u d o z
f d u z e t t u o c d a r
a o r i r h r l t t i r n
s e n u x r r o o i a r e
t n i d a o e n r o a d a
e x t r a o r d i n a r y
s c u o n m r o z o l f x
t o r o r h x n e r n r a
o u e d s p e e d o r e o
x c t a r a i u a o e r e
n h e t d e o n u o n x p
e u s b u o i n r u e c e
```

Largest Golf Tee

Photo: Guinness World Records Limited

Students in Escanaba, Michigan, built a golf tee that measured 26 ft. 8 in. (8.13 m) long with a head diameter of 35 in. (88.9 cm) and a shaft width of 13.87 in. (35.24 cm).

Did You Know?
One billion golf balls lined up side by side could circle the Earth along the equator.

ACTIVITIES

1. *Homophones* are words that sound alike but have different meanings and spellings. The words *tee* and *tea* are homophones. Write two more homophones you know.

   _____   _____

2. The largest golf tee is 26 feet long. Fill in the missing numbers in this pattern.

   2, 6, 10, _____, _____, 22, _____

Most Apples Bobbed in One Minute

Ashrita Furman (USA) bobbed 33 apples in one minute in Jamaica, New York, on February 19, 2008.

Photo: Guinness World Records Limited

Did You Know?
Jonathan Chapman, nicknamed "Johnny Appleseed," hiked through the Ohio and Indiana wilderness planting apple seeds for future settlers.

ACTIVITIES

1. Look at the apples below. Circle the first and fourth apples. Draw an X through the third apple. Draw a worm in the second apple.

2. Furman bobbed 33 apples in one minute. How many apples could he bob in four minutes?

_____

3. What is your favorite autumn activity?

_____

Largest Alphorn Ensemble

Photo: Guinness World Records Limited

On August 20, 2009, an alphorn ensemble consisting of 366 musicians played various songs on the Gornegrat Mountain near Zermatt, Switzerland.

Did You Know?
Early alphorns were used to communicate with flocks of sheep, herds of dairy cows, other shepherds, and villagers.

ACTIVITIES

1. A group of 366 people played alphorns. What is $\frac{1}{2}$ of 366?

   _____

2. What is $\frac{1}{3}$ of 366?

   _____

3. Since ancient times, alphorns have been used to send signals and warnings. Make up a sound you and a friend can use to signal each other. Describe your sound and its meaning.

   _____

Most Coconuts Pierced With One Finger in 30 Seconds

Ho Eng Hui (Malaysia) successfully pierced four coconuts with one finger in 30 seconds in Johor Bahru, Malaysia, on June 21, 2009.

Photo: Guinness World Records Limited

Did You Know?
Monkeys can be trained to pick coconuts from trees, collect them, and load them onto cargo trucks. One monkey can harvest 700 to 1,000 coconuts each day.

ACTIVITIES

1. Ho Eng Hui pierced four coconuts in 30 seconds. How many could he pierce in five minutes?

_____

2. How many could he pierce in one-quarter minute?

_____

3. Some people think coconuts are nuts, but they are really seeds. Some people think tomatoes and pumpkins are vegetables, but they are really:

_____

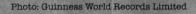

Chad Fell (USA) blew a bubble gum bubble with a diameter of 20 in. (50.8 cm) on April 24, 2004, in Double Springs, Alabama.

Photo: Guinness World Records Limited

Did You Know?
Double Bubble Bubble Gum was distributed as a military ration during World War II.

ACTIVITIES

1. There are over 1,000 flavors of gum in the United States. Some flavors are berry mint and cherry lemonade. Invent a new gum flavor.

   _____

2. The average person chews about 182 sticks of gum per year. Beginning at age five, about how many sticks of gum have you chewed in your lifetime?

   _____

Panel — page 11

ACTIVITIES — AMAZING BODIES

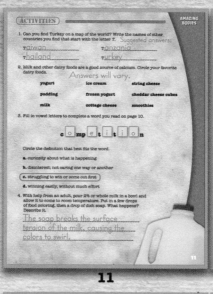

1. Can you find Turkey on a map of the world? Write the names of other countries you find that start with the letter T. **Suggested answers:**
Taiwan   Tanzania   Thailand   Turkey

2. Milk and other dairy foods are a good source of calcium. Circle your favorite dairy foods. **Answers will vary.**

yogurt   ice cream   string cheese
pudding   frozen yogurt   cheddar cheese cubes
milk   cottage cheese   smoothies

3. Fill in vowel letters to complete a word you read on page 10.

c o m p e t i t i o n

Circle the definition that best fits the word.
a. curiosity about what is happening
b. disinterest; not caring one way or another
c. struggling to win or come out first
d. winning easily, without much effort

4. With help from an adult, pour 2% or whole milk in a bowl and allow it to come to room temperature. Put in a few drops of food coloring, then a drop of dish soap. What happens? Describe it.
The soap breaks the surface tension of the milk, causing the colors to swirl.

11

Panel — page 14

Most Concrete Blocks Broken With the Elbow While Holding a Raw Egg

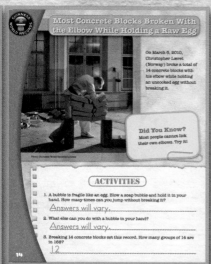

On March 6, 2010, Christopher Læret (Norway) broke a total of 14 concrete blocks with his elbow while holding an uncooked egg without breaking it.

Did You Know? Most people cannot lick their own elbows. Try it!

ACTIVITIES

1. A bubble is fragile like an egg. Blow a soap bubble and hold it in your hand. How many times can you jump without breaking it? Answers will vary.
2. What else can you do with a bubble in your hand? Answers will vary.
3. Breaking 14 concrete blocks set this record. How many groups of 14 are in 168? 12

14

Panel — page 17

ACTIVITIES — AMAZING BODIES

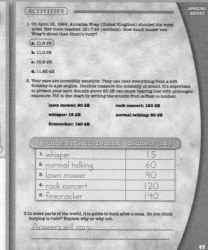

1. On April 16, 1994, Annalisa Wray (United Kingdom) shouted the word quiet. Her voice reached 121.7 dB (decibels). How much louder was Wray's shout than Hunn's burp?
a. 11.8 dB
b. 11.0 dB
c. 10.9 dB
d. 11.82 dB

2. Your ears are incredibly sensitive. They can hear everything from a soft footstep to a jet engine. Decibels measure the intensity of sound. It's important to protect your ears. Sounds above 85 dB can cause hearing loss with prolonged exposure. Fill in the chart by writing the sounds from softest to loudest.

lawn mower: 90 dB   rock concert: 120 dB
whisper: 15 dB   normal talking: 60 dB
firecracker: 140 dB

Sounds: Softest to Loudest	Decibels (dB)
1. whisper	15
2. normal talking	60
3. lawn mower	90
4. rock concert	120
5. firecracker	140

3. In some parts of the world, it is polite to burp after a meal. Do you think burping is rude? Explain why or why not. Answers will vary.

17

Panel — page 21

Tallest Girl

On January 16, 2009, Malee Duangdee (Thailand) measured 6 ft. 10 in. (2.08 m) tall in Bangkok, Thailand.

Did You Know? When Malee was just 12 years old, she was already 6 ft. 2 in. (1.87 m) tall, nearly a foot taller than her father.

ACTIVITIES

1. Give Duangdee's height in inches. 82 inches
2. Ask a friend to measure your height. How many inches tall are you? Answers will vary.
3. Compare your height to Duangdee's. How many inches taller is Duangdee? Answers will vary.

21

Panel — page 23

ACTIVITIES — AMAZING BODIES

Complete the crossword puzzle with words you read on page 22.

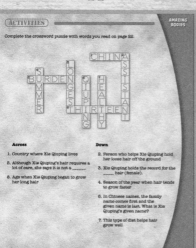

Crossword answers: CHINA, SUMMER, BURDEN, LONGEST, QIUPING, HEALTHY, THIRTEEN, ASSISTANT

Across
1. Country where Xie Qiuping lives
5. Although Xie Qiuping's hair requires a lot of care, she says it is not a _____
8. Age when Xie Qiuping began to grow her long hair

Down
2. Person who helps Xie Qiuping hold her loose hair off the ground
3. Xie Qiuping holds the record for the _____ hair (female).
4. Season of the year when hair tends to grow faster
6. In Chinese names, the family name comes first and the given name is last. What is Xie Qiuping's given name?
7. This type of diet helps hair grow well

23

Panel — page 26

Most Fingers and Toes on a Living Person

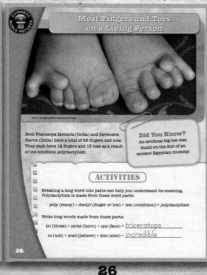

Both Pranamya Menaria (India) and Devendra Harne (India) have a total of 25 fingers and toes. They each have 12 fingers and 13 toes as a result of the condition polydactylism.

Did You Know? An artificial big toe was found on the foot of an ancient Egyptian mummy.

ACTIVITIES

Breaking a long word into parts can help you understand its meaning. Polydactylism is made from these word parts:

poly (many) + dactyl (finger or toe) + ism (condition) = polydactylism

Write long words made from these parts:

tri (three) + cerat (horn) + ops (face) = triceratops
in (not) + cred (believe) + ible (able) = incredible

26

Panel — page 27

Most Eggs Crushed With the Head in One Minute

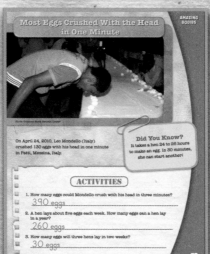

On April 24, 2010, Leo Mondello (Italy) crushed 130 eggs with his head in one minute in Patti, Messina, Italy.

Did You Know? It takes a hen 24 to 26 hours to make an egg. In 30 minutes, she can start another!

ACTIVITIES

1. How many eggs could Mondello crush with his head in three minutes? 390 eggs
2. A hen lays about five eggs each week. How many eggs can a hen lay in a year? 260 eggs
3. How many eggs will three hens lay in two weeks? 30 eggs

27

Panel — page 29

ACTIVITIES — AMAZING BODIES

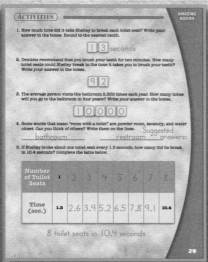

1. How much time did it take Shelley to break each toilet seat? Write your answer in the boxes. Round to the nearest tenth. 1.3 seconds
2. Dentists recommend that you brush your teeth for two minutes. How many toilet seats could Shelley break in the time it takes you to brush your teeth? Write your answer in the boxes. 92
3. The average person visits the bathroom 2,500 times each year. How many times will you go to the bathroom in four years? Write your answer in the boxes. 10000
4. Some words that mean "room with a toilet" are powder room, lavatory, and water closet. Can you think of others? Write them on the lines. **Suggested answers:** bathroom   restroom
5. If Shelley broke about one toilet seat every 1.3 seconds, how many did he break in 10.4 seconds? Complete the table below.

Number of Toilet Seats	1	2	3	4	5	6	7	8
Time (sec.)	1.3	2.6	3.9	5.2	6.5	7.8	9.1	10.4

8 toilet seats in 10.4 seconds

29

Panel — page 30

Most Clothespins Clipped on a Face

Garry Turner (UK) clipped 160 clothespins to his face on January 9, 2009, in Madrid, Spain.

Did You Know? Clothespins have been around for a long time. In the 1800s, 146 different kinds of clothespins were patented.

ACTIVITIES

1. Using a clothesline instead of an electric dryer can save a family $100 each year in energy costs. If 10 neighbors used clotheslines, how much would be saved in one year? $1,000.00
2. Some people love clotheslines because they save energy. Others think they are ugly and should not be used. What do you think? Answers will vary.

30

Longest Time to Hula-Hoop Under Water

AMAZING BODIES

Ashrita Furman (USA) Hula-Hooped under water for 2 minutes 38 seconds at an aquatic center in East Meadow, New York, on August 1, 2007.

Did You Know?
In four months in 1958, Wham-O sold 25 million of the first Hula-Hoop toy hoops for $1.98 each.

ACTIVITIES

1. Look around. How many things can you find that are shaped like a Hula-Hoop? List them.
   Suggested answers: a dinner plate, a bike wheel, a lampshade

2. With a friend, see who can keep a Hula-Hoop going the longest without letting it fall. How long did the winner keep going?
   Answers will vary.

31

31

Longest Time Holding a Vertical Person Overhead

AMAZING BODIES

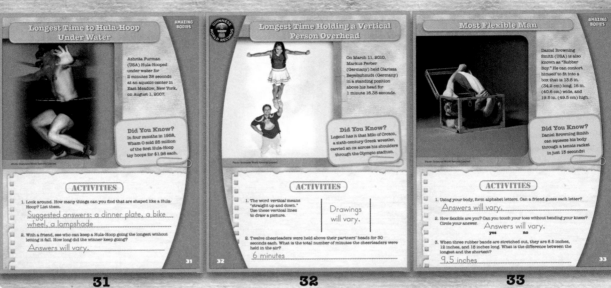

On March 11, 2010, Markus Ferber (Germany) held Clarissa Beyelschmidt (Germany) in a standing position above his head for 1 minute 16.38 seconds.

Did You Know?
Legend has it that Milo of Croton, a sixth-century Greek wrestler, carried an ox across his shoulders through the Olympic stadium.

ACTIVITIES

1. The word vertical means "straight up and down." Use these vertical lines to draw a picture.

   Drawings will vary.

2. Twelve cheerleaders were held above their partners' heads for 30 seconds each. What is the total number of minutes the cheerleaders were held in the air?
   6 minutes

32

32

Most Flexible Man

AMAZING BODIES

Daniel Browning Smith (USA) is also known as "Rubber Boy." He can contort himself to fit into a box that is 13.5 in. (34.2 cm) long, 16 in. (40.6 cm) wide, and 19.5 in. (49.5 cm) high.

Did You Know?
Daniel Browning Smith can squeeze his body through a tennis racket in just 15 seconds!

ACTIVITIES

1. Using your body, form alphabet letters. Can a friend guess each letter?
   Answers will vary.

2. How flexible are you? Can you touch your toes without bending your knees? Circle your answer.
   Answers will vary.

3. When three rubber bands are stretched out, they are 8.5 inches, 18 inches, and 18 inches long. What is the difference between the longest and the shortest?
   9.5 inches

33

33

ACTIVITIES

AMAZING BODIES

1. List four things people use to bind things together when making or repairing things.
   Answers will vary.

2. What does bind mean? Circle the best definition.
   a. to break apart
   b. to make curved or crooked
   c. to tangle up
   d. to fasten or hold together

3. Hold a ballpoint pen straight out from your stomach—that is about how far out Turner can pull his skin. How many inches is that? Mark it on the ruler.

4. Look around your home. List four things you find that stretch. What is the stretchiest thing you found? Circle it.
   Suggested answers:
   masking tape   nails
   rubber bands   screws

5. Draw a picture showing what you think you would look like with stretchy skin.

   Drawings will vary.

35

35

Fastest Time to Husk a Coconut

AMAZING BODIES

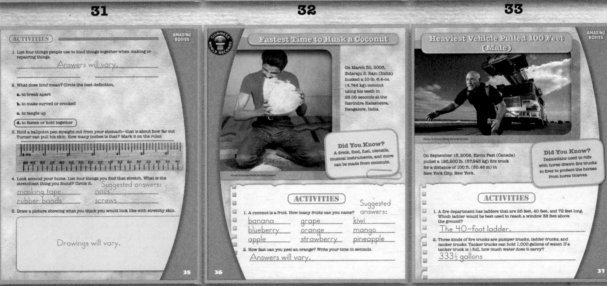

On March 30, 2003, Sidaraju S. Raju (India) husked a 10-lb. 6.4-oz. (4.744 kg) coconut using his teeth in 28.06 seconds at the Ravindra Kalashetra, Bangalore, India.

Did You Know?
A drink, food, fuel, utensils, musical instruments, and more can be made from coconuts.

ACTIVITIES

1. A coconut is a fruit. How many fruits can you name?
   Suggested answers:
   banana   grape   kiwi
   blueberry   orange   mango
   apple   strawberry pineapple

2. How fast can you peel an orange? Write your time in seconds.
   Answers will vary.

36

36

Heaviest Vehicle Pulled 100 Feet (Male)

AMAZING BODIES

On September 15, 2008, Kevin Fast (Canada) pulled a 126,200 lb. (57,243 kg) fire truck for a distance of 100 ft. (30.48 m) in New York City, New York.

Did You Know?
Dalmatians used to ride with horse-drawn fire trucks to fires to protect the horses from horse thieves.

ACTIVITIES

1. A fire department has ladders that are 25 feet, 40 feet, and 72 feet long. Which ladder would be best used to reach a window 36 feet above the ground?
   The 40-foot ladder.

2. Three kinds of fire trucks are pumper trucks, ladder trucks, and tanker trucks. Tanker trucks can hold 1,000 gallons of water. If a tanker truck is ⅓ full, how much water does it carry?
   333⅓ gallons

37

37

Heaviest Car Balanced on the Head

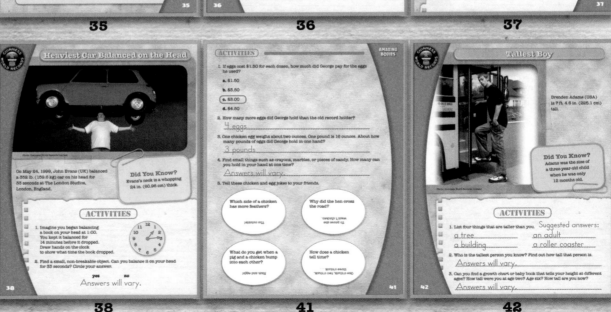

On May 24, 1999, John Evans (UK) balanced a 352 lb. (159.6 kg) car on his head for 33 seconds at The London Studios, London, England.

Did You Know?
Evans's neck is a whopping 24 in. (60.96 cm) thick.

ACTIVITIES

1. Imagine you began balancing a book on your head at 1:00. You kept it balanced for 14 minutes before it dropped. Draw hands on the clock to show what time the book dropped.

2. Find a small, non-breakable object. Can you balance it on your head for 33 seconds? Circle your answer.
   yes   no
   Answers will vary.

38

38

ACTIVITIES

1. If eggs cost $1.50 for each dozen, how much did George pay for the eggs he used?
   a. $1.50
   b. $3.50
   c. $3.00
   d. $4.50

2. How many more eggs did George hold than the old record holder?
   4 eggs

3. One chicken egg weighs about two ounces. One pound is 16 ounces. About how many pounds of eggs did George hold in one hand?
   3 pounds

4. Find small things such as crayons, marbles, or pieces of candy. How many can you hold in your hand at one time?
   Answers will vary.

5. Tell these chicken and egg jokes to your friends.

Which side of a chicken has more feathers?
The outside.

Why did the hen cross the road?
To prove she wasn't chicken.

What do you get when a pig and a chicken bump into each other?
Ham and eggs.

How does a chicken tell time?
One o'clock, two o'clock, three o'clock...

41

41

Tallest Boy

AMAZING BODIES

Brenden Adams (USA) is 7 ft. 4.6 in. (225.1 cm) tall.

Did You Know?
Adams was the size of a three-year-old child when he was only 12 months old.

ACTIVITIES

1. List four things that are taller than you.
   Suggested answers:
   a tree   an adult
   a building   a roller coaster

2. Who is the tallest person you know? Find out how tall that person is.
   Answers will vary.

3. Can you find a growth chart or baby book that tells your height at different ages? How tall were you at age two? Age six? How tall are you now?
   Answers will vary.

42

42

Shortest Stuntman

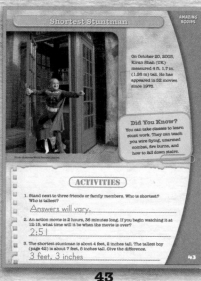

On October 20, 2003, Kiran Shah (UK) measured 4 ft. 1.7 in. (1.26 m) tall. He has appeared in 52 movies since 1976.

Did You Know?
You can take classes to learn stunt work. They can teach you wire flying, unarmed combat, fire burns, and how to fall down stairs.

ACTIVITIES

1. Stand next to three friends or family members. Who is shortest? Who is tallest?
   Answers will vary.

2. An action movie is 2 hours, 36 minutes long. If you begin watching it at 12:15, what time will it be when the movie is over?
   2:51

3. The shortest stuntman is about 4 feet, 2 inches tall. The tallest boy (page 42) is about 7 feet, 5 inches tall. Give the difference.
   3 feet, 3 inches

43

Most Pirouettes on Pointe on the Head

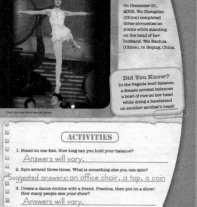

On December 31, 2006, Wu Zhengdan (China) completed three pirouettes on pointe while standing on the head of her husband, Wei Baohua (China), in Beijing, China.

Did You Know?
In the Pagoda bowl balance, a female acrobat balances a bowl of rice on her head while doing a handstand on another acrobat's head!

ACTIVITIES

1. Stand on one foot. How long can you hold your balance?
   Answers will vary.

2. Spin around three times. What is something else you can spin?
   Suggested answers: an office chair, a top, a coin

3. Create a dance routine with a friend. Practice, then put on a show! How many people saw your show?
   Answers will vary.

45

Most Pierced Man

As of October 17, 2008, John Lynch (UK) had 241 body piercings, including 151 in his head and neck.

Did You Know?
In ancient Egypt, only the pharaoh could have his navel pierced. Others might be executed.

ACTIVITIES

1. About how many piercings would Lynch have with 2.5 times as many? Round your answer to the nearest whole number.
   603

2. People in ancient Egypt may have been the first to use body piercings. The scarab beetle is a symbol used in Egyptian jewelry. Decorate this scarab beetle.
   Drawings will vary.

48

Most Eggs Crushed With the Wrist in 30 Seconds

On September 20, 2008, Balakrishnan Sivasamy (Malaysia) successfully crushed 25 eggs with his wrist in 30 seconds at a restaurant in Perak, Malaysia.

Did You Know?
The measurement of your arm, from your elbow to your wrist, is the same as the length of your foot. Check it out!

ACTIVITIES

1. Make a fun goal, like catching 20 balls or blowing up three balloons. Can you reach your goal in 30 seconds? Write what you did.
   Answers will vary.

2. The word egg has a double consonant, gg. List other words you know that have a double consonant.
   Suggested answers:
   bubble   success   funny
   llama   waffle   Mississippi

49

Most People Fire Breathing

On April 23, 2009, in Maastricht, Netherlands, 293 people breathed fire at the same time.

Did You Know?
October 9 is Fire Prevention Day, marking the date when Mrs. O'Leary's cow kicked over a lamp that started the Great Chicago Fire.

ACTIVITIES

1. To set this record, 293 people breathed fire. How many more people did this group need to reach 350?
   57 people

2. Write one way you can help prevent a fire at your home.
   Answers will vary.

3. Does your family have a place to meet outside in case of a fire? Write where you will meet.
   Answers will vary.

51

ACTIVITIES

Complete the statements by writing words you read on page 52. Then look in the puzzle to find the words you wrote. Search across and down.

Humans and other living things that have hair are __mammals__

Three bones inside the human ear are the __incus__, the __malleus__, and the __stapes__

The record holder for the longest ear hair is Anthony __Victor__

The most noticeable hair on humans is the hair on our __heads__

Anthony Victor has hair sprouting from the center of his outer __ears__

Victor is from the country of __India__

Victor's ear hair is about __seven__ inches long.

Toshi __Kawakami__ also has unusually long hair on his face.

Kawakami's __eyebrows__ are about seven inches long.

Kawakami is from the country of __Japan__

m	a	l	l	e	u	s	s	t
i	n	d	i	a	j	s	t	a
i	n	c	u	s	a	e	a	m
e	a	r	s	s	p	v	p	m
w	d	s	r	e	a	e	e	a
h	e	a	d	s	n	n	s	l
v	i	c	t	o	r	i	i	s
k	a	w	a	k	a	m	i	n
e	y	e	b	r	o	w	s	n

53

Longest Fingernails on a Male (Ever)

On May 30, 2009, Melvin Boothe's (USA) fingernails were a combined length of 32 ft. 3.8 in. (9.85 m).

Did You Know?
Another record holder, Shridhar Chillal (India), has not cut his fingernails since 1952. They are so long his wife gets up each night to turn him over.

ACTIVITIES

1. If the combined length of Boothe's 10 fingernails is 32 feet, what is the combined length of his fingernails on just one hand?
   16 feet

2. Fingernails grow four times as fast as toenails. If you trim your fingernails every week, how many times will you need to trim your toenails in one month?
   1 time

55

ACTIVITIES

1. Draw a line above the ruler to show the length of Taylor's tongue.

2. Stick out your tongue. Ask a friend to measure it from the tip to your closed top lip. Draw a line above the ruler to show the length of your tongue.
   Answers will vary.

3. Use your answer to #2. How much longer would your tongue need to grow to set the record for the world's Longest Tongue?
   Answers will vary.

4. The taste buds on your tongue detect four kinds of flavors. Write a favorite food for each flavor type.
   Answers will vary.
   Sweet: _____
   Sour: _____
   Bitter: _____
   Salty: _____

5. Your nose and tongue work together to taste foods. Try smelling a slice of onion while taking a bite of something else, such as an apple. What do you taste?
   Answers will vary.

59

Largest Tonsils

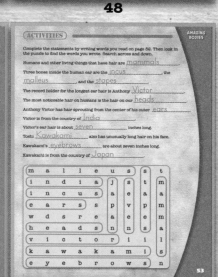

Justin Dodges (USA) had tonsils that measured 1.3 in. (3.2 cm) long, 1 in. (2.6 cm) wide, and 0.8 in. (2.1 cm) thick. They were surgically removed on December 18, 2008.

Did You Know?
Most six-year-old children's tonsils are larger than their parents' tonsils!

ACTIVITIES

Your tonsils can swell when you have a cold. Write letters to complete ways to take care of yourself when you are sick. Finish the sentence by writing the word formed by the circled letters.

d r i n k fluids
o v e r your mou t h
vi s i t the do c t o r
ea t hea l thy f o o ds

Most important: Get plenty of __rest__!

62

Heaviest Weight Pulled With the Eye Sockets

AMAZING BODIES

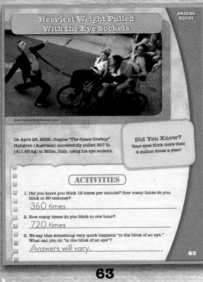

On April 25, 2009, Chayne "The Space Cowboy" Hultgren (Australia) successfully pulled 907 lb. (411.65 kg) in Milan, Italy, using his eye sockets.

Did You Know?
Your eyes blink more than 4 million times a year!

ACTIVITIES

1. Did you know you blink 12 times per minute? How many times do you blink in 30 minutes?
   360 times

2. How many times do you blink in one hour?
   720 times

3. We say that something very quick happens "in the blink of an eye." What can you do "in the blink of an eye"?
   Answers will vary.

63

63

Farthest Distance Limbo Skating Under Cars

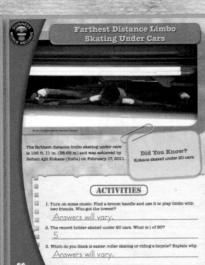

The farthest distance limbo skating under cars is 126 ft. 11 in. (38.68 m) and was achieved by Rohan Ajit Kokane (India) on February 17, 2011.

Did You Know?
Kokane skated under 20 cars.

ACTIVITIES

1. Turn on some music. Find a broom handle and use it to play limbo with two friends. Who got the lowest?
   Answers will vary.

2. The record holder skated under 20 cars. What is ¼ of 20?
   5

3. Which do you think is easier: roller skating or riding a bicycle? Explain why.
   Answers will vary.

66

66

Most Hugs Given in One Hour by an Individual

FANTASTIC RECORDS

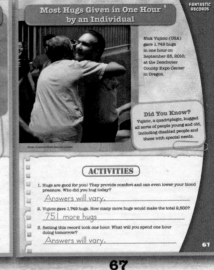

Nick Vujicic (USA) gave 1,749 hugs in one hour on September 25, 2010, at the Deschutes County Expo Center in Oregon.

Did You Know?
Vujicic, a quadriplegic, hugged all sorts of people young and old, including disabled people and those with special needs.

ACTIVITIES

1. Hugs are good for you! They provide comfort and can even lower your blood pressure. Who did you hug today?
   Answers will vary.

2. Vujicic gave 1,749 hugs. How many more hugs would make the total 2,500?
   751 more hugs

3. Setting this record took one hour. What will you spend one hour doing tomorrow?
   Answers will vary.

67

67

Fastest Half Marathon Running Backward (Female)

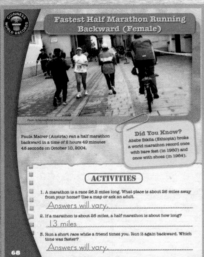

Paula Mairer (Austria) ran a half marathon backward in a time of 2 hours 49 minutes 45 seconds on October 10, 2004.

Did You Know?
Abebe Bikila (Ethiopia) broke a world marathon record once with bare feet (in 1960) and once with shoes (in 1964).

ACTIVITIES

1. A marathon is a race 26.2 miles long. What place is about 26 miles away from your home? Use a map or ask an adult.
   Answers will vary.

2. If a marathon is about 26 miles, a half marathon is about how long?
   13 miles

3. Run a short race while a friend times you. Run it again backward. Which time was faster?
   Answers will vary.

68

68

Most Heads Shaved in One Hour

FANTASTIC RECORDS

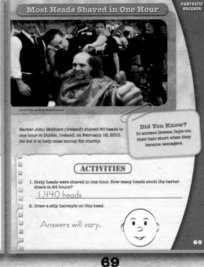

Barber John McGuire (Ireland) shaved 60 heads in one hour in Dublin, Ireland, on February 18, 2010. He did it to help raise money for charity.

Did You Know?
In ancient Greece, boys cut their hair short when they became teenagers.

ACTIVITIES

1. Sixty heads were shaved in one hour. How many heads could the barber shave in 24 hours?
   1,440 heads

2. Draw a silly hairstyle on this head.

Answers will vary.

69

69

ACTIVITIES

FANTASTIC RECORDS

1. Finkle carved 40 pumpkins after 20 minutes. How many pumpkins did he carve per minute?
   2 pumpkins

2. The world's Heaviest Pumpkin weighed about 1,810 pounds. If an average pumpkin weighs 10 pounds, how many average pumpkins would it take to weigh the same as the Heaviest Pumpkin?
   181 pumpkins

3. During his world record attempt, Finkle beat his original goal of carving 70 pumpkins and pushed himself to go further. Write about a time when you accomplished a goal and then pushed yourself to achieve even more. How did it make you feel?
   Answers will vary.

4. Draw happy, silly, wacky, or scary faces on these pumpkins.

Drawings will vary.

71

71

Fastest Time to Crawl One Mile

The fastest time to crawl one mile (1.6 km) is 23 minutes 45 seconds and was set by Suresh Joachim (Canada) in Toronto, Ontario, Canada, in 2007.

Did You Know?
Some babies crawl forward on their hands and knees, but others crawl backward, scoot on their bottoms, or roll.

ACTIVITIES

1. Run a short race in different ways while a friend times you. Try running, crawling, jumping, and skipping. Which way of moving was the fastest?
   Answers will vary.

2. The record holder crawled for one mile in about 23 minutes. Could he crawl for two miles in one hour? Circle your answer.
   yes   no

72

72

Longest Marathon on a Seesaw

FANTASTIC RECORDS

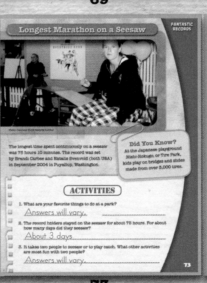

The longest time spent continuously on a seesaw was 75 hours 10 minutes. The record was set by Brandi Carbee and Natalie Svenvold (both USA) in September 2004 in Puyallup, Washington.

Did You Know?
At the Japanese playground Nishi-Rokugo, or Tire Park, kids play on bridges and slides made from over 3,000 tires.

ACTIVITIES

1. What are your favorite things to do at a park?
   Answers will vary.

2. The record holders stayed on the seesaw for about 75 hours. For about how many days did they seesaw?
   About 3 days

3. It takes two people to seesaw or to play catch. What other activities are most fun with two people?
   Answers will vary.

73

73

Fastest Mile Balancing a Soccer Ball on the Head

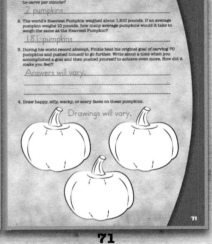

On March 20, 2010, Yee Ming Low (Malaysia) ran a mile in 8 minutes 35 seconds while balancing a soccer ball on his head.

Did You Know?
In many cultures, people carry heavy loads on their heads. Children even carry stacks of school books that way.

ACTIVITIES

1. How many steps can you take while balancing a ball on your head?
   Answers will vary.

2. How many feet are in one mile? Use a reference book or a Web site to find the answer.
   5,280 feet

3. What is your favorite sport to play with a ball?
   Answers will vary.

74

74

Longest Marbles Playing Marathon

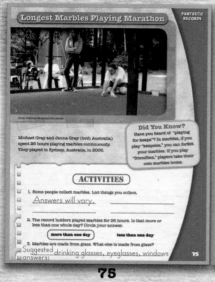

Michael Gray and Jenna Gray (both Australia) spent 26 hours playing marbles continuously. They played in Sydney, Australia, in 2008.

Did You Know?
Have you heard of "playing for keeps"? In marbles, if you play "keepsies," you can forfeit your marbles. If you play "friendlies," players take their own marbles home.

ACTIVITIES

1. Some people collect marbles. List things you collect.
   Answers will vary.

2. The record holders played marbles for 26 hours. Is that more or less than one whole day? Circle your answer.
   more than one day   less than one day

3. Marbles are made from glass. What else is made from glass?
   Suggested answers: drinking glasses, eyeglasses, windows

75

ACTIVITIES

1. A penny is ⅔ of an inch wide. It would take 16 pennies to form one foot. There are 5,280 feet in a mile. How many pennies would it take to form one mile?
   84,480 pennies

2. Find Honduras on a map. What continent is it on? Is it in the northern or southern hemisphere?
   North America; Northern hemisphere

3. If 85,000 pennies were used in setting this world record, how many dollars were used? Circle the answer.
   a. $8,500.00
   b. $850.00
   c. $8.50
   d. $85,000.00

4. Look for pennies around your home or school. Collect them all for one week. How many did you find?
   Answers will vary.

5. Toss a penny and catch it in the palm of your hand 10 times. Fill in the chart to show your results.

Toss	1	2	3	4	5	6	7	8	9	10
Heads or Tails?				Answers will vary.						

6. Flip the coin one more time. Predict whether it will land on heads or tails. Was your prediction correct?
   Answers will vary.

77

Fastest Mile Balancing a Baseball Bat on a Finger

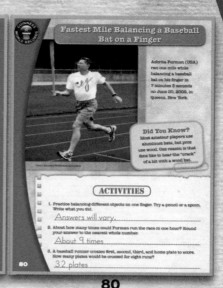

Ashrita Furman (USA) ran one mile while balancing a baseball bat on his finger in 7 minutes 5 seconds on June 20, 2009, in Queens, New York.

Did You Know?
Most amateur players use aluminum bats, but pros use wood. One reason is that fans like to hear the "crack" of a hit with a wood bat.

ACTIVITIES

1. Practice balancing different objects on one finger. Try a pencil or a spoon. Write what you did.
   Answers will vary.

2. About how many times could Furman run the race in one hour? Round your answer to the nearest whole number.
   About 9 times

3. A baseball runner crosses first, second, third, and home plate to score. How many plates would be crossed for eight runs?
   32 plates

80

Most Skips on a Unicycle in One Minute

Daiki Izumida, also known as Shigeyari (Japan), skipped rope while on his unicycle 214 times in one minute in Hong Kong, China, on August 12, 2007.

Did You Know?
Engineers are studying how unicycles work to help invent new one-wheeled personal mobility devices.

ACTIVITIES

1. How many times can you skip rope in one minute?
   Answers will vary.

2. The record holder skipped 214 times in one minute. How many times could he skip in 15 minutes?
   3,210 times

3. The word part uni means "one." Write uni on the lines to make words.
   uni cycle   uni verse
   uni corn   uni son

81

Complete the crossword puzzle with words you read on page 82.

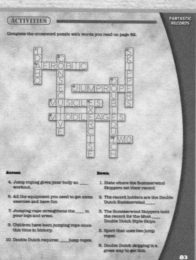

Across
4. Jump roping gives your body an ____ workout.
5. All the equipment you need to get some exercise and have fun.
7. Jumping rope strengthens the ___ in your legs and arms.
9. Children have been jumping rope since this time in history.
10. Double Dutch requires ____ jump ropes.

Down
1. State where the Summerwind Skippers set their record.
2. The record holders are the Double Dutch Summerwind ____.
3. The Summerwind Skippers hold the record for the Most Double Dutch Style Skips.
6. Sport that uses two jump ropes.
8. Double Dutch skipping is a great way to get this.

83

Most Cartwheels in One Minute

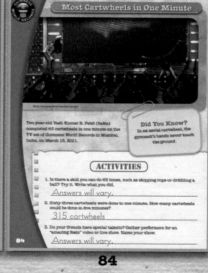

Ten-year-old Yash Kumar R. Patel (India) completed 65 cartwheels in one minute on the TV set of Guinness World Records in Mumbai, India, on March 15, 2011.

Did You Know?
In an aerial cartwheel, the gymnast's hands never touch the ground.

ACTIVITIES

1. Is there a skill you can do 65 times, such as skipping rope or dribbling a ball? Try it. Write what you did.
   Answers will vary.

2. Sixty-three cartwheels were done in one minute. How many cartwheels could be done in five minutes?
   315 cartwheels

3. Do your friends have special talents? Gather performers for an "amazing feats" video or live show. Name your show.
   Answers will vary.

84

Most Consecutive Chin-Ups

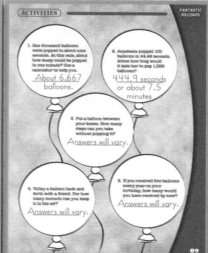

At age 70, Lee Chin-Yong (Korea) did 612 consecutive chin-ups. He completed them in 2 hours 40 minutes in Seoul, South Korea, on December 29, 1994.

Did You Know?
Taekwondo, a martial art, is one of the most popular activities in Korea. Its name means "art of the hand and foot."

ACTIVITIES

1. The record holder did 612 chin-ups. What is ⅓ of 612?
   204

2. What does the saying "keep your chin up" mean?
   To stay hopeful and optimistic

3. What is your favorite way to play and exercise using the muscles in your arms?
   Answers will vary.

85

Most Glasses Balanced on the Chin

Ashrita Furman (USA) balanced 81 drinking glasses (20 oz. each) on his chin for 12.10 seconds in Jamaica, New York, in 2007.

Did You Know?
If you have good balance, thank your cerebellum. That part of the brain at the back of the head controls movement and coordination.

ACTIVITIES

1. The record holder balanced 81 drinking glasses. What is the square root of 81?
   9

2. Drinking water is important, especially when you exercise. How many glasses of water did you drink today?
   Answers will vary.

3. What small, unbreakable object can you balance on your chin?
   Answers will vary.

87

ACTIVITIES

1. One thousand balloons were popped in about nine seconds. At this rate, about how many could be popped in one minute? Use a calculator to help you.
   About 6,667 balloons.

2. Anastasia popped 100 balloons in 44.48 seconds. About how long would it take her to pop 1,000 balloons?
   444.9 seconds or about 7.5 minutes

3. Put a balloon between your knees. How many steps can you take without popping it?
   Answers will vary.

4. Volley a balloon back and forth with a friend. For how many seconds can you keep it in the air?
   Answers will vary.

5. If you received five balloons every year on your birthday, how many would you have received by now?
   Answers will vary.

89

Fastest 10 Meters Balancing a Cue Stick on the Chin

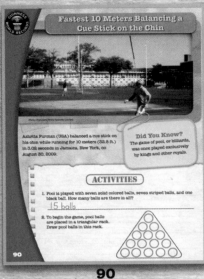

Ashrita Furman (USA) balanced a cue stick on his chin while running for 10 meters (32.8 ft.) in 3.02 seconds in Jamaica, New York, on August 30, 2009.

Did You Know?
The game of pool, or billiards, was once played exclusively by kings and other royals.

ACTIVITIES

1. Pool is played with seven solid colored balls, seven striped balls, and one black ball. How many balls are there in all?
   15 balls

2. To begin the game, pool balls are placed in a triangular rack. Draw pool balls in this rack.

90

Most Balloons Inflated by the Nose in Three Minutes

FANTASTIC RECORDS

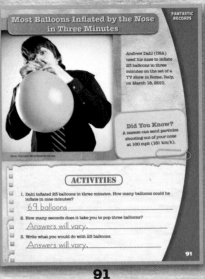

Andrew Dahl (USA) used his nose to inflate 23 balloons in three minutes on the set of a TV show in Rome, Italy, on March 18, 2010.

Did You Know?
A sneeze can send particles shooting out of your nose at 100 mph (161 km/h).

ACTIVITIES

1. Dahl inflated 23 balloons in three minutes. How many balloons could he inflate in nine minutes?
   69 balloons

2. How many seconds does it take you to pop three balloons?
   Answers will vary.

3. Write what you would do with 23 balloons.
   Answers will vary.

91

Most Push-Ups in 12 Hours

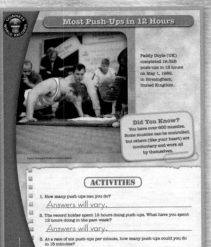

Paddy Doyle (UK) completed 19,325 push-ups in 12 hours on May 1, 1989, in Birmingham, United Kingdom.

Did You Know?
You have over 600 muscles. Some muscles can be controlled, but others (like your heart) are involuntary and work all by themselves.

ACTIVITIES

1. How many push-ups can you do?
   Answers will vary.

2. The record holder spent 12 hours doing push-ups. What have you spent 12 hours doing in the past week?
   Answers will vary.

3. At a rate of six push-ups per minute, how many push-ups could you do in 15 minutes?
   90 push-ups

92

Fastest Mile Hula-Hooping While Balancing a Milk Bottle on the Head

FANTASTIC RECORDS

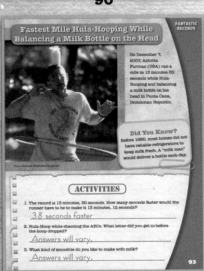

On December 7, 2007, Ashrita Furman (USA) ran a mile in 13 minutes 50 seconds while Hula-Hooping and balancing a milk bottle on his head in Punta Cana, Dominican Republic.

Did You Know?
Before 1950, most homes did not have reliable refrigerators to keep milk fresh. A "milk man" would deliver a bottle each day.

ACTIVITIES

1. The record is 13 minutes, 50 seconds. How many seconds faster would the runner have to be to make it in 13 minutes, 12 seconds?
   38 seconds faster

2. Hula-Hoop while chanting the ABCs. What letter did you get to before the hoop dropped?
   Answers will vary.

3. What kind of smoothie do you like to make with milk?
   Answers will vary.

93

ACTIVITIES

1. During Bradák's world record attempt, he successfully juggled three balls, catching them 1,876 times. What is ½ of 1,876?
   938

2. Look at your answer to #1. Are you able to toss and catch a ball that many times? Circle your answer.
   yes   no   Answers will vary.

3. Do you like to watch people juggling? Explain why or why not.
   Answers will vary.

4. Find the Czech Republic and the Netherlands on a map. Are the two countries close to each other? Which country would you rather visit? Why?
   Answers will vary.

5. Learning to juggle takes time and practice. Read the steps below for juggling three balls. Number the steps in order from 1–6.
   5 Repeat steps 1–4.
   1 Hold two balls in your right hand and one ball in your left hand. Toss ball #1 from your right hand.
   3 As ball #2 reaches the top of the arc, toss ball #3 from your right hand up and underneath ball #2. Catch ball #2.
   4 Catch ball #3.
   2 As ball #1 reaches the top of the arc, toss ball #2 from your left hand up and under ball #1. Catch ball #1.

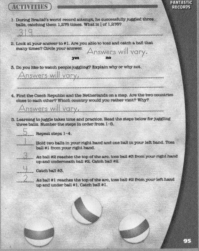

95

Longest Duration Balancing on One Foot

Arulanantham Suresh Joachim (Sri Lanka) balanced on one foot for 76 hours 40 minutes in May 1997.

Did You Know?
Why do flamingos stand on one foot? It may be that keeping one foot out of the water helps them conserve body heat.

ACTIVITIES

1. How long can you balance on one foot? Have a friend time you.
   Answers will vary.

2. For about how many days did the record holder balance on one foot?
   About 3 days

3. What is the tree pose in yoga? Ask an adult or use a Web site to find out.
   In tree pose, you stand on one foot with the other foot resting beside the opposite knee. The arms are raised overhead.

96

Most Two-Finger (One-Arm) Push-Ups in One Minute

Mohammed Mohammed Ali Zeinhom (Egypt) did 46 two-finger push-ups in one minute in front of the Giza Pyramids in Cairo, Egypt, on March 8, 2010.

Did You Know?
The push-ups were done using the pointer finger and thumb.

ACTIVITIES

1. Forty-six push-ups took one minute. About how many could be done in 15 seconds? Round to the nearest whole number.
   12 push-ups

2. Try brushing your teeth using only two fingers. Was it easy or difficult? Why?
   Answers will vary.

98

Longest Basketball Dribbling Marathon

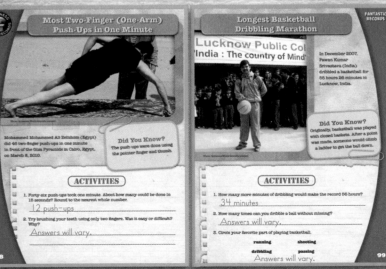

In December 2007, Pawan Kumar Srivastava (India) dribbled a basketball for 55 hours 26 minutes in Lucknow, India.

Did You Know?
Originally, basketball was played with closed baskets. After a point was made, someone would climb a ladder to get the ball down.

ACTIVITIES

1. How many more minutes of dribbling would make the record 56 hours?
   34 minutes

2. How many times can you dribble a ball without missing?
   Answers will vary.

3. Circle your favorite part of playing basketball.
   running   shooting
   dribbling   passing
   Answers will vary.

99

ACTIVITIES

FANTASTIC RECORDS

1. Write a sentence using the word unlimited.
   Answers will vary.

2. Going at the same pace as he did during his world record attempt, how many grapes could Furman catch in his mouth in five minutes?
   425 grapes

3. Grapes are a healthy snack. Circle your favorite healthy snacks. Put a star beside the fruits.
   Answers will vary.
   banana ⭐   cheese and wheat crackers
   yogurt   cereal
   grapes ⭐   carrot sticks
   peanut butter and celery   apple slices ⭐

4. Furman set his very first record by doing 27,000 jumping jacks. Count how many jumping jacks you can do before you get tired. Color in one star for each 10 jumping jacks you complete.
   Answers will vary.
   ⭐⭐⭐⭐⭐
   ⭐⭐⭐⭐⭐

101